The Life of a Nepali Village Boy

The Life of a Nepali Village Boy

AMBIKA MOHAN JOSHEE

A PEACE CORPS WRITERS BOOK

The Life of a Nepali Village Boy
A Peace Corps Writers Book - an imprint of Peace Corps Worldwide

Printed in the United States of America
By Peace Corps Writers of Oakland, California

For more information, contact peacecorpsworldwide@gmail.com.
Peace Corps writers and the Peace Corps Writers colophon
are trademarks of PeaceCorpsWorldwide.org.

ISBN: 978-1-950444-18-2
Library of Congress Control Number: 2020924404

First Peace Corps Writers Edition, June 2021

Dedication:

To my mother, Putali Maya Joshee; my wife, Kamala Joshee;
and our whole family.

You can run away from these surroundings, from this environment, and from your school for a day or two, but you can't run away from your life and from this world. Life is full of struggle. You have to struggle to survive. If you can't adapt, there will be very little chance for you to have a decent life.

—My mother, Putali Maya Joshee

Contents

Foreword

Growing Up Together

It was a great pleasure to read this autobiography of one my best friends—Ambika. Biographies have always been one of my favorite genres to read. In earlier times, biographies or autobiographies were written by or for famous philosophers, politicians, and rulers. Autobiographies written by lesser known commoners like me is quite a recent phenomenon. In this context, Ambika's *The Life of a Nepali Village Boy* is a great addition.

Ambika, Mohan Kayastha, and I are almost of the same age. We grew up together on a side street of Bandipur. Our mothers were friends. This brought us closer; we went to school, played, and did our schoolwork together most of the time. Our parents were struggling to get some financial stability, and soon they moved to different towns. We were separated even before we were teenagers. We continued our education in different towns. Soon after we completed the tenth grade, known as school leaving certificate (SLC), both Ambika and I started looking for jobs. Since none of us were interested in being involved in family businesses or other occupations, we had no choice but, as Ambika says in this book, to grab whatever would come our way. Eventually both of us became teachers/headmasters.

The main features of Ambika's professional life are quite vividly highlighted in the earlier chapters of this book. After being involved with several US-based training programs for Peace Corps/Nepal, I joined Peace Corps as a language officer in Nepal. During our various conversations, Ambika expressed his interest in being involved in Peace Corps/Nepal. An opportunity came in 1971 when I could invite him to work as a language instructor and cultural informant in a training program for new volunteers. None of us had anticipated that this would lead him to work there at PC/N for thirty years, slowly and gradually stepping up the ladder of success. This was possible because of his strong will to do better as well as his diligence and dedication in his work and efforts. Ambika is truly an achiever.

Ambika, in one of the chapters when he was a student at an elementary school in Bandipur, mentions that he had difficulty in getting interested in his education. But as he tried different jobs in the beginning of his career, he clearly saw that it is education that opens up all possibilities in life. This conviction continued and didn't stop until he completed his PhD at the age of seventy-four. Now he strongly believes that education is a lifelong process and that everybody can and should continue learning in a formal or nonformal way.

Ambika's strong family support also contributed a lot to his success in life. His mother, like my mother, was illiterate or semiliterate but always provided encouragement and moral support to continue his education. His wife, Kamala, a dear friend of mine, and his lovely and bright daughters have always tried to provide an environment that was conducive to fulfill his quest for education and the desire to succeed in his work.

After he retired from the Peace Corps, with his daughters already in the US, he could have easily settled down in the US to do his PhD at one of the better-known universities there. Yet he chose to do it in Nepal. He knew that many educators here could learn a lot from his different researches that he had done in preparation of his thesis. Ambika is a good patriot.

At the end of this foreword, I want to say without any hesitation that this book, *The Life of a Nepali Village Boy*, will greatly inspire students of any level and professionals in any sector to make every effort to improve the quality and relevance of Nepal's education system.

—Chij K. Shrestha
Kathmandu, Nepal

Foreword

The Strands of a Strong Cord

"Everyone has a story." This is one of our main observations sitting in airport lounges or bus terminals. Ambika Joshee proves this point in this book through vignettes about his life in Nepal that are interesting, important, and often humorous.

When Ambika was a boy, Nepal was called a less developed country. In his lifetime, dim evenings lit by lanterns gave way to computers in schools and ubiquitous smart phones. The oral traditions in thousands of remote villages in dozens of local languages gave way to the national language of commerce, government, radio, and television. These kinds of massive changes, some not without controversy, are perhaps best exemplified by the arc of Ambika's own education from a primary class with six young students to a PhD from an admirable university in Dhulikhel, Nepal.

From 1963 through 1973, I was involved with the Peace Corps in Nepal, initially as a volunteer. Yet, it was only in 1991 that I met Ambika, a long-serving member of the Peace Corps staff. With the gift of distance, I began to ponder how he came to that position.

Maybe the answer is the strands of a strong cord of his character, including curiosity, talent, and responsibility. His stories carry these themes. He was curious about other people, places, and cultures, hoping to find common threads with the life lessons of his mother. He was talented: able to secure work, develop schools, and convince others to aid these selfless efforts, especially in education. And he was responsible: responsible to the farmers in the co-ops he led, responsible to the students he taught, responsible to the volunteers he prepped and supported, and responsible to his family above all. His work touched the lives of thousands.

I was gratified to learn that Ambika, a lovely man and a born teacher and diplomat, had decided to share his life story. To anyone interested in South Asia, in human development, or in determination without many tools, this book will bring smiles, knowledge, and inspiration.

—Will Newman

Tiverton, Rhode Island

Preface

Incidents happen. They come and go, but some remain in our memory for life. I will never forget some of these incidents. These are memories of my childhood, my school life, my working days, my retirement life, and my quest for knowledge in retired life. These are the memories of my nearly eight decades of life.

People say when you retire, you look for an easy life. I felt I was not tired even when I retired from my full-time job. I was always looking for something to do. Kamala (my wife) and Jharana and Archana (my two daughters) were the sources of my inspiration. I took full-time or part-time jobs, did social work, and returned to school after I retired. All these activities gave me tremendous joy. I got to meet new people and make new friends from different age groups. It was interesting being in the same class with colleagues who were four decades junior to me. Interacting with different age groups compelled me to learn how they think and to change myself to fit into their environment.

The majority of my working life was spent as the associate Peace Corps director for education (APCD/Ed) of US Peace Corps/Nepal. The United States of America is a mosaic of people who have migrated from different parts of the world at different times. In my thirty-plus years of involvement with the Peace Corps, I came across volunteers from various age groups, ethnicities, political views, and sexual orientations. Some of the memories are reflective of the diversity of the Peace Corps volunteers and the differences in their adaptation to the local culture. When two cultures meet, the conflux sometimes produces surprising results. Sometimes the results become the accepted norms, and sometimes they become grounds for revolution. The Peace Corps volunteers came with their own views of the world, so adapting to a new culture was certainly not easy for them. For me, it was both a challenge and a pleasure, as I enjoy working with people from diverse cultures.

Goethe once said, "All writing is confession." However, I write neither to confess the activities of my past nor to promote my political or philosophical views. Many of the incidents that I recount in this memoir happened as part of the flow of life, and I have nothing to confess or hide. They do not always represent my views but instead are the thoughts that came to my mind when the incidents occurred. These incidents are not uniquely illuminating, but they may show readers how life was in those days. People who were involved in these incidents may find it amusing to see them from a different perspective.

Most of these stories came out when I was sharing my experiences with Jharana and Archana. I was trying to familiarize them with life in those days and also to give them some examples of what kind of results we can expect when people of two cultures meet in different environments, different settings, and different surroundings. In this memoir I wander through politics, culture, education, religion, and many more realms.

Names, places, and dates have been changed in most cases to maintain anonymity. Dates are either changed or not mentioned so as not to disclose the identities of people involved in the incidents. Some of these incidents could have been seen differently from the perspectives of the others who were involved, but I have tried to pen them as I felt when the incidents took place.

I am not a writer by profession, and I have tried to minimize my authorial presence. I do so in the hope that my experience and my observations will shed some light for the readers and not carry them away beyond the experiences and observations. This book is a mixed bag of my experiences with people from different backgrounds and their experiences from my perspective.

I apologize to all who may have different views about these experiences. Credit goes to all who were somehow involved in this memoir. If anyone feels misrepresented, it's my fault. Mea culpa.

—Ambika

Acknowledgments

The inspiration for this memoir came from inside the family. When I talked about my workdays to my daughters, most of the time they laughed and sometimes they found what I said to be unbelievable, and they encouraged me to jot down what I was telling them. They convinced me that it could be interesting to many, whether they are returned Peace Corps volunteers (RPCVs) or the new generation of Nepali youth or my colleagues from different periods and different situations in my life. My sincere thanks go to my daughters, Jharana and Archana—*un abbraccio* (a hug). Both of them pushed me to distill my experiences into a memoir. I would also like to thank both of them for their untiring work of proofreading this book during their busy schedules.

The understanding of my wife, Kamala, while I was sitting with my laptop cranking out my thoughts before I lost a sequence, meanwhile not minding my household chores, was a strong show of encouragement. She was another force pushing me from behind to complete this work. A warm hug.

A sincere thanks goes to Dr. Ann Sturley, for taking the time to read my crude version of the memoir and accepting the tiresome work of editing it. Her deep experiences from her working days in Nepal, her interactions with Peace Corps volunteers and staff, and her cultural experiences from different parts of the world certainly helped to produce this memoir in this format. Thank you, Ann.

Thank you to my friends Will Newman and Chij K. Shrestha for agreeing to write forewords for this booklet on short notice. Thank you also to my friend James Pesout (RPCV/Nepal) for taking time to read my manuscript and giving me valuable suggestions.

—Ambika

The Life of a Nepali Village Boy

Early Days

Introduction

I was born in a small Newari town, Bandipur, situated in western Nepal.

I came from a lower-middle-class family. My high school education was interrupted many times because the school often closed for months due to political differences among the Bandipures. My friends from well-off families went to Kathmandu and other cities to complete their high school and higher education, but I had to wait in Bandipur until the high school opened again. Two of my close friends, Chij Shrestha and Mohan Kayastha, went to Kathmandu and completed their high school (School Leaving Certificate Examination: SLC) in 1959 and 1960, respectively, whereas I remained in Bandipur and completed my SLC in 1961. I was in Bandipur only until I finished high school. Immediately after I finished high school at tenth grade, I moved to Narayangarh, Chitawan, where some of my family members had moved a few years before. In my high school and college days, I was not the best student in my class. I did all my college studies at home and took my exams privately, as I was a full-time employee throughout my college years. In Nepal, most students get full financial support from the family for their college or university education, but I was an exception because of financial constraints.

My father had a good business in Bandipur. He had a big cloth store in partnership with another Bandipur family. There were just a few years of this easy life. Later on, the business failed, and my father moved to Gorakhpur in India, a town with many Nepalese who had settled there after their active life in the Indian army. He took another wife in Gorakhpur, and we were left in Bandipur without any support. I appreciate my mother's bold and courageous attitude to life during that time; she helped us grow up with pride and provided for our education. It was not easy for a single woman to raise six children. She also fought a legal battle in court with my father's partner to save whatever little property we had left at that time. When I was younger, I never understood the grand effort she put in for me and my siblings. To this day, I still don't know how she did it. She encouraged us to go for higher education as far as we could.

When I was in high school, I did many odd jobs to support my education and also to support my family. My mother was again the source of inspiration. Even now I see my childhood friends who didn't complete high school, living in Bandipur with bare-bones income from traditional, old-style subsistence farming on small land holdings acquired from their parents, but my mother guided me to pursue an academic path. She is still a big force in my life, and she continues guiding me even though she is not in this world anymore.

Growing up in the small towns of Bandipur in Tanahu district and Narayangarh in Chitawan district, I faced many surprises when I first visited Kathmandu when I was fourteen. I had never seen an indoor toilet. We were used to outhouses in Chitawan and Bandipur. I had never seen a telephone until I went to Kathmandu. The first time I saw a lift (elevator) in my life was at the Hotel Taj in Bombay (Mumbai) on a trip to Beirut for a conference. I saw a computer for the first time in my life while working for Peace Corps. Our administrative officer brought in the computer, put it on my desk, told me to start using it, and said that he would arrange a basic training later on. These were just a few of the many new experiences for this simple village boy.

Guru Mantra

This incident took place when I was seven years old. I was living in Bandipur, and it was just a month before the Revolution of 2007 BS (1951 AD) against the Rana regime in Nepal. The residents of Bandipur played a vital role in this revolution. Seven people from the area sacrificed their lives to set the country free from the Rana tyranny.

My father was in Gorakhpur, India, doing retail business at that time. His store mainly attracted Gorkha soldiers from the Indian army. My elder brother was also in Gorakhpur, studying for his matriculation examination. At home in Bandipur, six of our family members remained: my mother, two elder sisters, one younger sister, my younger brother, and me.

I was studying in elementary school at that time. Studying was not one of my favorite activities. I used to escape school with any excuse that I could find. The teachers would give us homework of some simple math and two or three pages of handwriting. Most days I went to school without my homework and was punished. Corporal punishment was the teachers' favorite way to discipline their students.

In the farming season, my mother and my elder sisters worked on the farm, and I had to stay home to look after my younger siblings and prepare evening food for the family. That was a very good excuse for me not to go to school. Child labor was not an issue at that time. I was merely seven years old when I was performing these duties.

One day, early in the morning, I was looking for an excuse not to go to school. My excuses were not working, so I told my mother that I was going to go to school, but instead I decided to go to my maternal uncle's village, Mahibal. It was about a four-hour walk away, and there was no road to Mahibal in those days. I left home with a friend of my own age, pretending that I was going to go to school. We reached my uncle's house around 5:00 p.m. My friend also had relatives in the same village whom he would visit, so it worked out well for both of us. My uncle was surprised but at the same time very happy to see me. He was surprised because we had no adults accompanying us on that four- or five-hour trek from Bandipur to Mahibal. He asked me several questions about the situation at home and why I had come alone without any family member. I was so tired I ate dinner early and went to bed.

The next day, early in the morning, my uncle sent a man to Bandipur to inform my mother that I was in Mahibal. That first day in Mahibal passed very pleasantly. No pressure to study. No questions about anything. Free to play all day and eat good food. I was very happy. I could not have asked for more. I noticed that in the evening, the older folks got together at my uncle's house to chat and smoke. A *chilim* (clay bowl) was placed at the top of a *hukkah*, and a long rubber tube was joined to the lower part of the *hukkah*. I noticed that they put some tobacco in the *chilim* and that the *chilim* was filled with burning coals. That was only for the grown-ups, and I was not allowed to have a puff. Rather, my uncle would ask me to refill the tobacco and coal in the *chilim* from time to time. It looked fascinating to see those grown-up people smoking and letting the smoke come out of their mouths.

The following day, when nobody was home and all the family members went to their farm, I decided that I was going to try to smoke the *hukkah*. I had seen people preparing it, and I had refilled it many times, so I had no problem preparing it. In the evenings, five or six people would take turns smoking, but that afternoon I was alone, and I kept smoking until there was no tobacco smell. I was all right for a while, but after fifteen or twenty minutes, I felt nauseated and dizzy and went outside the house and vomited. After a while I went to bed and slept.

In the evening, when everybody came back home from the fields, they were surprised to see me in bed. They asked me what was wrong.

When they figured out what I had done, that was the end of my happy life in Mahibal.

The next day, my uncle gave me a notebook and asked me to write six or seven pages and do some simple math every day. As I could not avoid what I was trying to escape in Bandipur, I did not see any reason to stay in Mahibal anymore. My uncle also saw I was not showing any interest in my studies, so he decided to send me back to Bandipur. This time he would not let me go without an adult. He hired a person to go to Bandipur with me. Once I was back in Bandipur, I had no choice but to go to school regularly.

Immediately after I came back from this trip, my mother told me, "You can run away from these surroundings, from this environment, and from your school for a day or two, but you can't run away from your life and from this world. Life is full of struggle. You have to struggle to survive. If you can't adapt, there will be very little chance for you to have a decent life." My mother could barely read and write her name. She could not do arithmetic on paper, but she had a calculating machine in her brain. She was a strong woman. She had experienced all the trouble she could have faced in her life. She had seen her husband slipping away from her. She had seen poverty and all the problems she had to go through feeding and raising her six children as a single parent. I can imagine where those strong and powerful words were coming from. In her rosy days, she had experienced the benefits of her husband being a government employee and being considered a wise person.

Even though she did not have a chance to read Charles Darwin's book *On the Origin of Species* or know about Herbert Spencer's phrase "survival of the fittest," she still put pressure on us to succeed. While Darwin received great acclaim for his theory of natural selection in the midnineteenth century, Russell Wallace was wandering around New Guinea, Malaysia, and Indonesia collecting samples to prove that species change according to changes in the environment. Wallace was too poor to even finish grammar school but nevertheless was able to further the theory of evolution. Similarly, my mother was barely literate, but she intuitively understood the survival of the fittest and was able to plant the seed of the value of education in my head.

All these theories were foreign to her. But our mother always reminded us that "education is the key that opens doors to opportunities." She thought education would become still more important in the future. She had wished to educate all her children but was successful only in persuading her male children to go for higher education. None of the three daughters went beyond high school.

My mother even applied her love of education to herself. Decades after my fateful trip to my uncle's village, she—a nonagenarian lady—never got tired of practicing writing her name in Devanagari script and would spend hours trying to decipher a children's book.

When I was young, I don't know how much I appreciated my mother's words. But now, every word she said at that time inspires me. She taught me the importance of the battle of survival and how to fight it. She taught me to persevere and do my work sincerely and diligently. She taught me how to survive in this world. She taught me that all the people on this planet are equal and that nobody should be looked down upon based on their material possessions and their physical appearance. She taught me that only my inner soul knows if I am doing the right things the right way. I have used these lessons whenever I have had to make hard decisions. Without her magic words, I don't know where I would be or what I would be doing now. She knew exactly what she was planting in my head.

My mother was the untiring *guru* (teacher) of my life who explained to me in my childhood every step necessary for my future life. This was my *guru mantra* (sacred words). The lessons I learned from her carry more weight than all the books I have read in my life. My mother's view was to aim high, to never look down on people, to treat others the way you would like to be treated, and to make decisions by asking your inner soul if it is a fair decision. These mantras have worked very well for me in my professional life. Whenever I have had to make a hard decision, I would sit down quietly for a moment and ask myself what is right and what is wrong in each of the possible choices. People might not agree with my decisions, but I have never regretted following my mother's word because I knew I was making unbiased decisions.

Even now, I often look at her picture and bow my head to her. *Pranam* to my mother and to the guru of my life, who gave me the encouragement to survive and lead a successful life in this competitive world.

An Audience with the King

Bandipur is seven kilometers south of Dumre Bazaar, which is on the Kathmandu-Pokhara highway. It is a small hilltop settlement with a population of about sixteen thousand. About 1,030 meters (3,380 feet) above sea level, it is situated on a saddle of the Mahabharat range. It is a beautiful town with old Newari architecture. All the houses have slate roofs, and the bazaar has been paved with slate. To preserve the town's character, motorized vehicles are not allowed into the town center. It is a living museum of Newari culture. This traditional architecture is also found in all the temples. Most of the Newars migrated from Bhaktapur, outside Kathmandu, and they brought their architectural knowledge with them. The Bandipur bazaar used to be a trade center supplying merchandise to various villages of Tanahu, Lamjung, Mustang, Manang, Kaski, Palpa and Shyangja districts of western Nepal. The massive flood of 1954 forced many people from those districts, and businessmen from Bandipur settled in the flatlands of Chitawan.

Bandipur in the early days

The government's transfer of the district center from Bandipur to Damauli played a vital role in encouraging the migration of Bandipures to Dumre and Damauli. The then prime minister, Surya Bahadur Thapa, took political revenge on the Bandipures by transferring the district headquarters from Bandipur to Damauli. We call the prime minister in this case a *Sakuni,* referring to a character in the Mahabharat whose advice to take revenge against the Pandavas created misfortune. Another blow to Bandipur was wielded in building the Prithvi Highway, which connects Narayangarh and Pokhara not through Bandipur but instead around the hill below Bandipur, making it a deserted town.

Now the town is slowly developing as a hub for nearby tourist spots and also as an education center with a college, two high schools, one middle school, and several elementary schools. Slowly, small agricultural and other home-based industries have begun popping up, improving the economy of the area. The Bandipur Social Development Committee (BSDC) has played a vital role in the development of Bandipur. Chij Kumar Shrestha, Dr. Madan Piya, Iswor Gopal Pradhan, and many others have played an important role in bringing Bandipur to its current state. BSDC is a nonprofit nongovernmental organization (NGO) based in Kathmandu that conducts fund-raising, infrastructure development, and other activities to help Bandipur gain its old fame. Bandipures residing in Kathmandu have helped Bandipur come to today's condition through financial donations and other social contributions.

Deserted Bandipur town in the 1970s

Bandipures in North America (BNA), an organization for which I was the founding president from 2009 to 2012, has also supported Bhanu High School through financial contributions. We funded the building and furnishing of one room in the extension building of the school.

Bandipur is a politically conscious town. In my high school days, the youths were divided into two groups, the Congress Party and the Communist Party. The town played an important role in the revolution against the Rana regime in 2007 BS (1951 AD). Seven locals were killed by the Rana militia in that confrontation and were dragged and thrown from the hill above the *tundikhel*. The next day, local people found the bodies and buried them properly. The place where they have been buried has been named Martyrs' Park.

Bandipur after restoration

Bandipur has a strong yet strange history of education. A public library was started during the Rana period. Adhar School, which prepared students for basic trades and cottage industries, was also started around that time. An elementary school was also established around the end of the Rana regime. Bhanu High School was founded immediately after the collapse of the Rana regime. Bhanu High School was a small school located next to the *tundikhel,* at the northwest end of Bandipur bazaar. Almost all the students were from Bandipur. Most were Newars from the local bazaar. There were about six or seven students in our class. Almost all the teachers were local except a few from Kathmandu. Most of the local teachers only had a high school degree. Since Bandipur was a remote village, educated people did not want to come from Kathmandu, as jobs were abundant in Kathmandu in those days.

Once in a while, the school management committee members went to Kathmandu to recruit teachers for Bhanu High School. Conflict between local people of differing political orientations hampered the high school's operation time and again. At times the school was closed just because two groups of people could not come to an agreement—not on educational philosophy but on decisions about the infrastructure of the school, the hiring and firing of teachers, or the financial matters.

At one time, Bandipur had two different high schools just because of politics. The Congress Party and the Communist Party each had their own separate schools. The Congress Party succeeded in taking the existing school building in *tundikhel,* and the Communist Party started their own school in Tin Dhara. There was no way to sustain two high schools for three to four hundred households. Awareness of the need for education was very low outside the bazaar. People would rather send their kids to herd cattle and/or keep them home to take care of their siblings rather than send them to school. Bandipures tried their best to sustain both of the schools, going from house to house to raise funds for them. They requested *mutthi dan*—requesting that the townspeople put aside a *mutthi* (fistful) of rice for the school before each meal. Sustaining two high schools in Bandipur was not easy. Finally, the Bandipures decided to give up their disagreement for the sake of educating their children and merged the two schools.

If I remember correctly, I was in sixth grade at that time. It was just before the beginning of the Panchayat system. King Mahendra was making tours around the country. As soon as the rumor came that the king had planned a visit to Bandipur, the youths and schoolteachers planned a drama to show him. Shivaram, Debi Lal, and Bhuban Lal were some of the teachers responsible for the drama initiative. Krishna Bhai, Om Kumar, Prem Binod, Madan Mohan, and others were also involved. I was an actor in the drama. The drama was about the Revolution of 2007 BS (1951 AD), and we used firecrackers to replicate gunfire during the revolution in Bandipur. While we were performing for the king, someone came onstage and told us that we were being rounded up by the army—just like prisoners. We were clueless as to why the army was concerned. We had no idea that we had to ask their permission to use firecrackers because we were showing the drama to the king. The army commander came onstage and asked us many questions that we could not answer. He then realized our ignorance and let us continue the drama. It was a new and strange experience for us.

Bandipures were and still are very much interested and enthusiastic about educational development. The affluent and elite people of the bazaar often sent their male offspring to Kathmandu, looking for the best education for their children. Others had to depend on whatever education facility was available there. The existing facilities were very crowded, and the building was in a dilapidated state, showing the need for bigger and better school facilities. The people realized the need for new facilities and started discussions. Hira Lall and Shyam Krishna Pradhan donated a plot of land to build a school at the foot of Gurungche danda, and the construction funds were collected from the local residents. The managing committee decided to request the king to lay the foundation stone of the school building while he was in Bandipur for his visit. When the king agreed to lay the foundation stone, the managing committee started raising funds to make sure that the school had enough money to complete the building. At the same time, the local people were also expecting some financial help from the government.

The program was set. Around noon, the king went to the new school ground with his entourage. A fine stage, according to Bandipur standards, was made. The place was decorated with flowers, and colored triangular flags made of paper were attached to strings. The whole town gathered to have a look at the king. The kings were seen as an incarnation of Lord Vishnu, and people had the belief that one look at the king would open their door to heaven.

We had a small Nepal Scouts team at the school. The scout committee assigned me to tie a scout scarf around the king's neck on the stage. Everything went as planned, and I was called to the stage at the proper time. I had never been in front of any dignitaries before. I was sweating even before I approached the stage. I had the scout scarf in my hand, and I presented the scout salute as soon as I climbed the small ladder to the stage. Then I slowly marched forward and stopped when I was just about a foot or two from the king. Everything was going as I had been taught by my teachers until I started tying the scout knot. My hands started shaking, and I was having a problem even getting the scarf around his neck. I spent about five minutes trying to make the knots, but I had no luck. He was smiling and kept quiet. He did not say a single word. He was just looking at me, which also made me nervous. After about five minutes, when the Aide-de-camp (ADC) general saw that I had not succeeded in tying the knot, he told me, "Just leave it. It is all right. You don't have to tie the knot."

Experience as a Teenager

The consequences of the Second World War were still present. Except for food grains, all supplies had to come from India. My father's cloth store at the heart of Bandipur was well established. He was running it in partnership with another local person from the town. They went to India at least once a year to get their supplies for their stores. Nepali currency had a very high value at that time, as it was made of pure silver. Paper money had just started to be in circulation. People preferred coins over paper money. The businesspeople would wait for the people coming on leave while serving in the Indian army, to exchange money with them. If they could not get enough Indian currency, then they would take Nepali coins to India, and they got a good exchange rate.

At one point my father went to India for a business trip. We did not have any information about him for several weeks. Then, all of a sudden, we learned that he had taken a woman as his second wife and had started a small business in Gorakhpur. We were devastated, and this was when our most difficult days started. My father's business partner took advantage of the situation and became the sole owner of the business. He filed a case at the court saying that my father had taken a huge sum of money with him when he went to India, demanding that he be compensated from our private property for the money and for the decline of the business suffered after my father left.

Our financial situation became dire. My mother had to take care of her six children without any source of income. My maternal uncle, Babu Lal Shrestha (my mother's brother), came to our rescue many times during these unstable times. At one point, my older brother decided to go to Gorakhpur to find our father. I followed him after several months. My brother decided to stay in Gorakhpur with our father and his second wife, where he completed high school at Maharana Pratap Intermediate College, currently Maharana Pratap University. I also went to this intermediate college (which also ran elementary and secondary classes) and studied there up to sixth grade.

I was there for about two years, until our father decided to return to Nepal. My brother and I went directly to Bandipur, and my father and his new wife decided to go to Narayangarh. Bhanu High School did not have many students, as most of the students were from Bandipur itself. Very few students came from neighboring villages, and still fewer were from the neighboring districts. I enrolled in sixth grade, which only had seven or eight students.

Among them, three of the boys were Chij, Mohan, and me, and the three girls were Laxmi, Bombay, and Chhunu. Most of the teachers were local residents of Bandipur. My brother taught at Bhanu High School for few years and then went to Narayangarh, but I stayed in Bandipur until I finished high school. I took my SLC examination in 1961, and then I also went to Narayangarh.

Among my classmates of those days, Chij Kumar Shrestha worked for Peace Corps for many years and then worked as country director (Nepal) and vice president as well as Asia director for World Education Inc., Boston. Chij introduced me to the Peace Corps. Mohan Bahadur Kayastha worked for Nepal Electricity Authority for many years, retired as a senior officer, and then started his new life as an author, which was his passion. He has published more than fifty books. Laxmi Shrestha completed her bachelor's degree and was in government service for a long time. Mandodari (Bombay) Pradhan and Kesh Kumari (Chhunu) Pradhan got married after high school and settled with families.

After my SLC, I had a sequence of different jobs. My brother and my maternal uncle, Babu Lal Shrestha, helped me start a convenience store named Joshi and Shrestha Circle. It went well for a while but did not last. After that we started a soap factory making laundry soap. The factory was going well, but many of the factory workers quit because their skin was breaking down due to the caustic soda (sodium hydroxide). We did not have modern machinery to work with the caustic materials, so we had to close our factory even though demand for our product was high in the local market.

My brother had started teaching at Chitwan High School, the only high school in the district at that time. One person's salary was not enough for our whole family to *haat mukh jodnu* ("to put hand and mouth together," meaning to be able to eat). I decided I also wanted to teach. I went to talk to the School Managing Committee chairman. He said he was willing to hire me if I would teach Sanskrit. I think he did not want to hire me, which was why he gave me such a difficult offer, but I accepted the Sanskrit teaching job. It was not easy. I had a poor background in Sanskrit language and literature. I used to spend the whole morning preparing myself for the school day. Luckily, they found a Sanskrit teacher within a few months, and I was assigned to teach geography in grades eight, nine, and ten.

As I did not know what I wanted to do in my life, and also due to necessity, I took whatever job came my way, doing varied jobs in my teenage years. It was good exposure to life, and these experiences opened my doors to the future.

Starting a High School

I was slowly settling into my teaching job, but I was not very happy, as the students were rowdy, and it was difficult to teach fifty-plus students in a classroom without any teaching materials except chalk and a blackboard. At the same time, I was doing self-study and preparing for my intermediate in commerce (I.Com.) examination. I had a dream of studying medicine, but our financial situation combined with my low high school grades compelled me to give up that dream. I took a three-month leave of absence from the school and went to Kathmandu to take the exam. I passed my I.Com. with flying colors, if I say so myself. Luckily, after I got my I.Com. results, there was an opening for the job of district cooperative manager at the Cooperative Union in Bharatpur. I was accepted and started working there.

This job gave me a chance to work with other government employees in the district. There were a lot of government office holders who had not finished high school but felt stymied since there were no schools in Chitawan where they could continue their education after office hours. These junior employees shared their ambition for higher education with me when we met for work-related discussions. In our informal tea-drinking meetings, this issue came up many times. We discussed that the people of Chitawan district appreciated the need for education and that new schools were being started. There were three or four high schools in the whole district by now, Chitawan High School being the first. However, there was still a need for a high school that working people could attend. Then, one day Chitawan High School headmaster Prem Kumar Shrestha; a local social worker, Ganesh Prasad Pandey (Ganesh Guru, who had a keen interest in the field of education); and I discussed the possibility of opening a night school for government employees. Diththa Rup Narayan Joshi, Subedar Tapta Bahadur Khatri, and many other local residents helped us in our endeavor.

A general meeting of the local residents of the Bharatpur area was called at Ganesh Prasad Pandey's residence. The outcome was that a night high school would start in the rudimentary thatched-roof structure of Bharatpur Rastriya Prathamik Vidyalaya (elementary school). We started with two students and three teachers. Balram Guru was the third teacher, along with Prem Kumar and me. As there was no electricity in the whole district at that time, we bought a few lanterns to start with. Essentials such as chalk, dusters, attendance registers, kerosene oil, and lanterns were bought with the money from the teachers' pockets. Shrestha was appointed headmaster, and I got the responsibility of assistant headmaster. Thus, I became one of the founding members of Shree Narayani Ratri (Night) High School, currently known as Narayani Higher Secondary School in Bharatpur, Chitawan.

The thatched-roof structure of the Bharatpur Elementary school premises where Narayani Ratri (night) High School was started with five classrooms and an office. We had a metal trunk where we stored all the school equipment. Sketch by Ram Hari Shrestha

One of the new school buildings that replaced the old Narayani Ratri High School structure, on a larger plot of land. Photo by Ram Hari Shrestha

We were surprised to find out that in addition to government workers, many farmers came to enroll in our school. They had given up their studies because they couldn't attend school during the day. Once people found out about the school, enrollment increased. The students included primary-level schoolteachers from the surrounding schools, nursing students from the nursing training center of Bharatpur Hospital, female volunteer health workers, and other employees of the government offices. We had a large number of government employees in our enrollment because Bharatpur was a district town center. Besides office employees, there were other students who had dropped out of school and were older than students in regular schools.

At the end of the first month, we decided to pay ourselves from funds that we had accumulated from the students' tuition fees. At that time, we had only two students, Prem Nidhi and Buddhi Sagar, so we had about thirty rupees. Even though our salary was set according to the government pay scale, we decided to distribute the money equally among the three of us. We decided to go for *khaja* (snacks) with that money. The day was the fifteenth of *Asar*, so we said we would celebrate with *dahi chiura* (yogurt and beaten rice) as our *khaja* of the day. The fifteenth of Asar is a dahi chiura day in Nepal. At the same time, two other friends came and joined us. We enjoyed our khaja, but we had to add some money from our own pockets to pay the bill, as our combined one-month salaries did not cover it.

We, the founders of the school, were encouraged by the growing number of students enrolling day after day. Slowly but steadily, the school was flourishing and taking the shape of a real school even though we were running it in a thatched-roof building belonging to another school. Today, Narayani Ratri High School has become one of the best schools in the district.

Headmaster Ambika Mohan Joshee

A Trip to Kathmandu

After Prem Kumar Shrestha resigned as headmaster of Narayani Ratri High School, Narayan Prasad Sharma was appointed in his place. Sharma had a full-time job in a government office, so working at our night high school was his second job. When he was transferred to Kathmandu, he resigned from the headmastership, and I became the acting headmaster. School was running well, but the Ministry of Education had not yet accredited it. Despite our constant follow-up, the Ministry of Education was slow in making decisions, and we had to suffer. Without accreditation, we were not permitted to conduct the SLC test qualifying examination. Examination time was approaching, and our students in tenth grade needed to take the exam. I asked the headmasters from other schools of the district if they would be willing to accept our students in their test examination, but due to local politics, they were hesitant to accept my proposal. I waited until the last minute, and after not seeing any positive move from other schools, I decided to put the issue in the hands of the school management committee.

I presented the case at both the school management committee meeting and also the schoolteachers' meeting, but both times I was told to figure out a way to manage it. They authorized me to take necessary actions, recognizing that the students should not suffer and should not lose the three years they had already spent preparing for the exam.

My last option was to obtain affiliation with one of the government-recognized schools, allowing the students to take the test examination at our own school. It was a big undertaking. We had been running our school for the last three years, and this was our first batch of students ready for their SLC examination. This was a very diligent group of students, and we were expecting several of them to pass their SLC examination in first division, which was very rare in those days for schools outside Kathmandu Valley.

The test examination had to be finished before the end of October so that the students would be able to register and participate in the final SLC examination, held in December. I gave it serious thought, and various names from the Ministry of Education came into my mind.

One of them was Nirmardan Basnyat. I had met him in Birgunj two years earlier while I was going through adult education training. Mr. Basnyat was there as a trainer from Kathmandu, and I found out that he was not only joint secretary at the Ministry of Education but that he also taught in a night school in Kathmandu. Durga Prasad Sharma was headmaster at the night shift of Durbar High School. We met occasionally with Mr. Basnyat for drinks and *bagedi* (small birds fried and eaten as appetizers) in the evening after the training classes were over. Bagedi is a specialty found in small family-run restaurants in Loharpatti street in Birgunj. One evening I told Mr. Basnyat about our school in Bharatpur. I explained that all our students were either government service holders or farmers, neither of whom could go to school during the daytime. He thought it was a noble effort.

The day after my meeting with my teaching staff, I decided to go to Kathmandu to work out some kind of deal with one of the high schools there for the test exam. It was already 5:30 p.m. when I boarded a bus to Hetaunda after work. That bus took me up to Hetaunda, and the next morning I had to catch a bus to Kathmandu.

August is the month when it rains the most in Nepal. It was raining from the early morning, and I was not sure if buses from Hetaunda to Kathmandu would be canceled because of the heavy rain. Part of the road from Bharatpur to Hetaunda was not paved, and most of the road looked more like mud puddles than a road. Frequent landslides and other hazards forced the driver to be very careful, and he was going very slow, under twenty kilometers per hour. I knew it was going to take more than five hours to get to Hetaunda. The rivers were swollen, and there were several places with no bridges, so the bus had to ford the river, which was especially dangerous due to the high current.

I was twenty-two years old, full of courage and vigor, not married but with a day job as a district cooperative manager and a night job as assistant headmaster at the night school. I wanted to continue my higher education. I had only passed the intermediate examination (equivalent to a high school degree in America). Since I had started at this school as the founding assistant headmaster and had worked many times as acting headmaster whenever there was no headmaster, I was ready to face any obstacle to achieve our goal. Much hard work had gone into gaining government recognition for the school, but with no success. For many months our monthly salary was not even enough for snacks for the day. All of us were in effect working as volunteer teachers. It was only possible because all of us either had full-time jobs in the government or had our own businesses or farms. It was a matter of prestige for us now to have our students appear in SLC examination.

I was exhausted when I got to Hetaunda. I directly went to a hotel and got a room for myself. As soon as I registered at the hotel, I had my *dal bhat* and went to my room. I was very hopeful that I would be able to persuade Mr. Basnyat to help us obtain government recognition for our school so that we would be able to conduct our own test examination in our own school. As a high-ranking Ministry of Education official, he could easily persuade other officials in the ministry to help our school. As the local schools did not want to work with us, it was a question of dignity of the school and me. We had to save face. I had worked hard and would not let it fail at any cost.

About 60 percent of our school's students were female. Most of the female students were nursing students, village women health workers, or primary schoolteachers. The nursing campus enrolled about fifty students a year for a three-year program to be assistant nurse midwives. These students had just passed eighth grade. Women health workers were working in the villages in the field of reproductive health and family planning. They had passed only sixth or seventh grade. The primary teachers were mainly normal training graduates who had completed eighth or ninth grade.

My full-time job as cooperative manager and running the night high school had kept me very busy. After three years, we accepted admissions for the tenth grade and also had our own students entering tenth grade. We had about ten students in tenth grade by that time. This trip had a significant value for the students' future and also for the reputation of the school.

First SLC Test Examination

On my way to Kathmandu, I was plotting what to say to Mr. Basnyat and thinking about how crucial it was for us to be able to enroll our students in his school. I had to convince him that we had a very good batch of students and that we would have very good SLC results. What were my other options if they declined to accept our students? Talk to some other people I knew? I was also thinking about going to the Ministry of Education to see if I could immediately manage to get government recognition of our school. I decided to go to the Ministry of Education first, and if that did not work out, then to approach the administration of the Durbar school night shift where Mr. Basnyat taught. The Ministry of Education flatly denied my request based on the grounds that they needed at least six months to get paperwork from Chitawan's district education office and the Regional Directorate of Education.

Now my only remaining option was to go see Mr. Basnyat and Mr. Sharma at the night school they ran in a building belonging to Durbar High School. I went directly to them and explained our situation. We talked about our school, our students, their background, and the need for them to take the SLC test exam. We had a long discussion as to how we would conduct the examinations, grade papers, and register students for the SLC examination. They graciously accepted my request and entrusted me with their questionnaires for all the test subjects, with the agreement that I would send all the "copies" (answer papers) to them after the examination. They would grade the copies and decide who passed. The students who passed would appear for the SLC examination under the name of their school, not Narayani Ratri High School.

It was a big achievement for me. Our teachers, the students, and the managing committee members were all happy with the arrangement. As soon as I came back from Kathmandu, we set about preparing our students for the examination.

The Second Audience with the King and Government Recognition of the School

After the exam, we still felt bad that we had not been able to send our students to take the SLC examination in our school's name. We didn't want our students to lose the opportunity again, and for this, we had to start working on it early in the year. We applied to the district education office to obtain formal recognition from the Ministry of Education. Our several months' toil did not bear any fruit. We were desperate and needed to do something to get the school recognized before the upcoming SLC exam.

We heard that King Mahendra was planning a hunting trip to Chitawan. Chitawan was well known as a place for hunting tigers and other wild animals. During the Rana regime, British royalty came to Nepal to go hunting in Chitawan. Rumor became fact, and the king came to Chitawan. On the last leg of his trip, his camp was set up near the Bharatpur airport. We still had not been successful in getting our school recognized. I went to see the chief district officer and the zonal commissioner, requesting an audience with the king so I could take this issue to him, but I did not succeed with either of them. I was very upset, still looking for a way to arrange an audience.

There was no telephone in the whole district of Chitawan in those days. There were only government wireless services in district headquarters. The wireless service used Morse code to transfer messages from one station to another. Only the operators were able to send and receive messages, and they had to transcribe the messages into Nepali for the recipients. The day before the king was going to fly out from Chitawan, the zonal commissioner sent his messenger with a message around noon to meet him immediately. The minute he saw me, he told me that I had an audience with the king at six that evening. I don't know what happened. Why did the zonal commissioner change his mind all of a sudden? Had the king somehow heard about our school? How did he manage to get this information? These questions were never answered. But we were happy we had gotten the chance to share our problem with the king.

The zonal commissioner told me that I must present myself before the king in *daura suruwal* (Nepali national dress), which I did not have. I went to downtown Narayangarh and had my daura suruwal made in three hours. The tailor was very helpful. Once I mentioned my situation, he agreed to do my work immediately and started working on my daura suruwal.

The minute I was summoned by the zonal commissioner, I gathered some of my schoolteachers and worked on the application that would be presented to the king. Once we agreed on the content of the document, I left the responsibility to one of the teachers to prepare it. The teachers worked hard and came up with a very impressive application, which they handed to me two hours prior to my audience with the king. I had some time to rehearse how I wanted to present it to the king.

I was at the gate at 5:30 p.m. It was the Panchayat era, and security was very strict. I had to go through several security checks before I was presented to the king. This time I was not as nervous as I had been when I was in sixth grade. Nonetheless, I was sweating and could not start for a few seconds. I had repeatedly rehearsed what I was going to say, and we had also prepared a written application within the few hours that we had. I knew I had to convince the king about the need for the night high school in Chitawan.

The tent was spacious and well lit. A few army officers were standing in the corner. It was the hot month of August, so the tent was arranged in a way that would let a nice breeze come in, but even then I was sweating. The king was sitting on a couch, and there was a small coffee table in front of him. I saw his smiling face, and it looked like he was waiting to hear from me.

I had only five minutes allotted for my presentation. The minute I got in front of the king, I bowed down and started explaining how the town's people had previously not been able to pursue higher education due to a lack of classes available in the evening. I explained how we had started essentially as volunteer teachers in a rudimentary thatched-roof structure. I also explained the problem we had had the previous year in arranging for our students to participate in the SLC examination. I told him about my trip to Kathmandu and our students' high caliber. I think I took about twenty minutes, because the ADC whispered in my ear at least five times that my time was up. During those twenty minutes, the king did not speak a single word but kept nodding his head as a sign that he was listening to me. I finally gave up. I had my application ready, and I started to hand it over to the king, but the king motioned me to give it to the ADC. I bowed down again and left. I was glad that even at that short notice, we had been able to prepare a written application. I was glad that I had fully explained the needs and the problems our school was facing. I just hoped that someone in the royal palace would read my application and take the necessary actions.

I was happy that I had had a chance to lay my problem down to the highest authority of the country. I could not have hoped for a better chance. This kind of opportunity was rare in those days, and my audience with the king was the talk of the town. Everybody was eager to see what the result would be. We were hopeful that we would get recognition sometime in the near future. The tenth-grade students were hoping that they would be able to take their test examination under the auspices of our own school.

About two weeks later, we were in a tea shop for our late-afternoon tea when a postman came and handed me a letter from the royal palace. I was still working as acting headmaster. We had no idea as to the content of the letter except that it was about our request for government recognition of our school. Because we were all so curious about the letter, we opened it right there at the tea shop. The letter was written to the Ministry of Education and mentioned our request for the government recognition of our school. At the end of the letter, it said, "Take immediate action to provide government recognition to the school, and write a letter to the school with a carbon copy of the letter to the royal palace office." Our happiness knew no bounds.

The news went all the way to the students even before our formal announcement. The next day we had a big party, inviting all the office heads of the district as well as our students. It was a big day in the history of the school!

Female Students at the Movie Theater

Our school was finally officially recognized. We had moved our school to Chitawan High School from Rastriya Prathmik Pathshala. We had had problems running the school in the primary school's thatched-roof structure and were happy to shift to Chitawan High School's concrete building. The monsoon rains and premonsoon heavy winds had been especially difficult in that location without proper walls. Teaching by the light of a Petromax (a kerosene lamp with a mantle) on windy nights was especially difficult. The Petromax flame was easily extinguished, and it took most of the office helper's time to keep it going.

As time passed, we started enrolling students in lower grades. We had started with grades nine and ten and then added students down to grade five. We now had six classes, from grade five through grade ten.

The Nepali education system had been deteriorating day by day. Most of the parents were illiterate and did not understand the value of education. People did not care much about knowledge but just wanted to have a certificate. They were more focused on getting certificates than learning. They did not care whether their children acquired any knowledge. It was the same with the test examination. Teachers had problems with both the students and their parents. The parents just wanted their kids to pass the text exam so they could appear for the SLC examination. The parents knew that just appearing for the SLC meant they could gain some sort of government position. But the schools knew they would lose their financial assistance from the government if a certain percentage of the students did not pass the SLC examination for three years in a row.

In all school-level examinations, cheating was rampant, and some teachers even helped students to cheat just to have a good percentage pass in their schools. Because I was very strict in monitoring the exam, I was threatened by students of various grades from my own school as well as by students from other schools who took the exam at our school (just as our students had taken the exam under the auspices of the Kathmandu school the year before).

The district education officer was concerned about the pressure coming to the teachers from the students and their parents. With the persuasion of the local teachers, Bhoj Bikram Rai, the district education inspector, called a meeting of all the high school headmasters of the district and discussed forming a district test board in the summer of 2025 Bikram Sambat (1969 AD). The district education inspector was nominated chairman of the board, and I was selected unanimously as the executive secretary of the board. The board decided to have one test exam for the whole district with one set of question papers. Sets of sealed question packets were dispatched to all the participating schools. The headmaster of each school, in the presence of the local police officer and the pradhan panch (village mayor), was instructed to open the packet just half an hour before the examination starting time.

It was also decided that the answer "copies" (examination booklets) would be collected after the exam every day and would be checked at the district center. We had rented an office and selected subject teachers who were invited to the office to check the exams. It was probably the first district-level test examination conducted by a board in Nepal. We were careful to keep the names of all the teachers who were involved in checking the exams confidential. Even food and lodging were arranged for the teachers for the whole week when they were checking the answers. This was done to maintain the anonymity of the teachers so that they would not have any problems from the students and their parents. The answer copy books were coded, and there were no names in the copy books while the teachers were checking them. Teachers did not know whose answers they were checking. After all the copies were checked, they were decoded and mark sheets were prepared.

Finally, after about ten days' hard work, we had the final test results, which we published at the same time in all the schools and at the test board office. We posted the results on the wall of the test board office around noon. The teachers were happy and relaxed after their days of hard work.

After the results, all the board members; the police inspector, who was the security in charge of the district; and some of the teachers involved in checking the test papers decided to go to see a movie in downtown Narayangarh for relaxation. I don't remember what movie it was, but I know it was a Hindi movie.

About halfway through the movie, we were told that there were about twenty girl students waiting for us outside to smear our faces black (black residue from earthen pots is mixed with oil to create a messy paint). We had not realized that all the girl students from a neighboring school had failed the examination. The girls probably thought it was some kind of planned discrimination toward them. Nothing had been planned. The teachers who were checking the copies did not even know the names and genders of the students. To avoid a big scene at the movie hall, the police inspector sent for police reinforcements. When the police arrived, they escorted us to our residences.

It was surprising to see how quickly the girls got the information and united to take action against us. The next day we called some of the parents of the girls we had seen at the movie hall and explained the process we had gone through in marking the copies. We even showed them some copies. Thankfully, they were satisfied.

Hotel Taj

It had been just a few months since I had become manager of the District Cooperative Union in Bharatpur. The Bharatapur District Co-operative Union office was in a small room on the front porch of the cooperative warehouse. I had an accountant, a clerk, a store manager, two office helpers, a driver and a helper working for me. There were also mill managers and mechanics under my supervision. Two Peace Corps volunteers were assigned to my office to work as junior technical assistants (JTAs) to help farmers in the use of chemical fertilizers, insecticides, improved varieties of seeds, and agricultural tools. The volunteers also helped translate the manuals for the insecticides and fertilizers from English to Nepali so that farmers would be able to use the chemicals properly.

Peace Corps volunteer Pete Andrews and Ambika inspecting a wheat field. Pete was assigned to the district agriculture office and helped us translate the literature.

USAID had planned a seven-week training course for cooperative officers of Nepal at the American University of Beirut (AUB), Lebanon. People had been selected from all over Nepal, and there were about sixteen participants. The participants' ages ranged from around the early twenties to the midsixties. It was a mixed bag of participants as far as caste, ethnicity, religion, and position, though all were in one way or other involved in the cooperative movement. Some were board members who dealt mainly with policy matters, and some were managers who were responsible for executing the decisions of the board as well as the day-to-day operations.

The District Cooperative Union, Chitawan had nearly seventy member societies from different parts of Chitawan. Some were credit and savings cooperatives, others were marketing cooperatives, and some were multipurpose cooperatives. In many cases, the cooperative system worked very well in its role as an agricultural bank, providing loans to the farmers and collecting their savings. The cooperatives also made insecticides, chemical fertilizers, improved varieties of seeds, and improved agriculture tools made available to the farmers at reasonable prices at the right time of year and helped take their products to market. Most of those cooperatives, though, are nonexistent today due to unscrupulous management practices, lack of proper government supervision, and the inspectors' tendency to financially profit from the system. The cooperative inspectors would collect installments from the societies and individuals, but instead of depositing the money in the union or the bank, they pocketed the money. The District Cooperative Union suffered, as well as all the member societies.

The District Cooperative Union owned and operated one store and two mills for rice, flour, and oil. One mill was in Fulbari, and the other was in Parbatipur. The store was in Bharatpur. It offered agriculture tools, seeds, insecticides, fertilizers, and consumable goods like sugar, rice and lentils.

To participate in the training course, we were invited to Kathmandu for an orientation program. First, we were given a multiple-choice

English test. There were participants who had double master's degrees, and some had just finished their SLC or intermediate exam. I was worried, but I passed the test. Then there was an orientation program in Rabi Bhawan, an enormous old Rana palace where the USAID office in Kathmandu was, and still is, located. I had never been inside such a big building in my life. Everything was new and exciting for me. The orientation program was to introduce us to Western society, such as greetings, how to use silverware and a Western toilet, and other things that were new to us. Many of our Kathmandu friends threw parties for us, congratulating us on our luck in having a chance to travel abroad.

The day came. We boarded the plane and headed for Beirut via Bombay (Mumbai). The airline provided us rooms at the Hotel Taj in Mumbai with dinner and transportation coupons to and from the airport.

We used our travel voucher to go to the hotel. Hotel Taj was one of the best hotels in India. I had never been to a hotel that elegant. We checked in, and the bellboy took our luggage to our rooms. We took the lift (elevator) to go to our rooms, which was a first for me.

After refreshing ourselves, we went to the restaurant for dinner. It was a fancy restaurant. One of our colleagues, Dilip Bannerji, wanted to show us he knew his way around. While we were having our soup, I noticed Dilip calling the waiter to complain about something. Later, he told us he liked the soup so much he wanted to have another bowl, but he did not want to pay for it. He showed the waiter a hair in the soup and got another bowl.

After a delicious dinner with ice cream and pie for dessert, we decided to have some drinks. We were astounded to find out that Mumbai was a dry city and that the local people could not have alcoholic beverages in the restaurant. We had to go to our rooms to get our passports to show them that we were Nepali, not Indian. It was a new experience for us, and we were learning how to acclimatize ourselves to the local situation.

Learning continues as life goes on.

Life with the Volunteers

The Peace Corps

The history of the Peace Corps began with presidential candidate John Fitzgerald Kennedy's (JFK's) address to approximately ten thousand students waiting for him until midnight on October 14, 1960, at the University of Michigan in Ann Arbor. This was where he first announced his idea of the Peace Corps. The idea behind the Peace Corps came from several people, including Minnesota Senator Hubert Humphrey. In June 1960, Senator Humphrey introduced a bill to send young Americans to third-world countries to combat poverty, hunger, illiteracy, and disease, and he introduced the name Peace Corps in that bill. JFK consulted respected academic Max Millikan, political pundit Chester Bowles, and others to help him outline the organization and its goals.

In JFK's inaugural speech he said, "Ask not what your country can do for you; ask what you can do for your country." This quote can be heard across the global Peace Corps program. The Peace Corps is an American volunteer program run by the US government. The Peace Corps' mission is to promote world peace and friendship by fulfilling three goals:

- To help the people of interested countries in meeting their need for trained men and women
- To help promote a better understanding of Americans on the part of the people served
- To help promote a better understanding of other people on the part of Americans

A Peace Corps volunteer must be an American citizen, preferably with a college degree, who is willing to work in a third-world country for a period of twenty-seven months, including three months of preservice training. Some volunteers with good farming, home science, or other skills were also selected. Volunteers could work in any organization in their host country, including government offices that were selected by the country staff with input from the local government officials. The Peace Corps claims to be an organization that provides equal employment opportunity.

The first Peace Corps director was Sargent Shriver, JFK's brother-in-law. Initially, the Peace Corps was present in only five countries, but during his tenure, Sargent Shriver developed programs in fifty-five countries with more than 14,500 volunteers. He served as the director from 1961 to 1966.

The Peace Corps grew rapidly until the 1990s, when numbers plateaued. In the first thirty-two years, more than 140,000 young Americans served in ninety-two countries (Shapiro, 1994). By 2016, a total of 225,000 volunteers had served worldwide in 141 host countries. Almost all were college graduates. To this day, the Peace Corps continues to address global needs in the areas of clean water, access to education, health education, information technology, small-business development, and other areas. Many returned Peace Corps volunteers (RPCVs) have risen to prominent national and international jobs, and five have served as Peace Corps directors, Carol Bellamy, Mark L. Schneider, Ronald A. Tschetter, Aaron S. Williams, Carrie Hessler-Radelet.

RPCV Dr. Josephine (Jody) Olsen was sworn in as twentieth director of Peace Corps in March 2018. Dr. Olsen was a visiting professor at the University of Maryland and has served the Peace Corps in various capacities. She served as a Peace Corps volunteer in Tunisia from 1966 to 1968. Much later, Dr. Olsen served as an external reviewer of my PhD thesis, "Perspective of Financing Higher Education in Nepal, A Qualitative Research." Going through my thesis page by page, she provided many good suggestions, including language, content of the subject matter, and technical suggestions on APA format.

Carol Spahn RPCV Romania (1994-1996), who also served as the country director in Malawi for five years took the helm of Peace Corps as an acting director from January 2021.

RPCVs can't be assigned to military intelligence duties for a period of four years following Peace Corps service. They are also prohibited for life from serving in military intelligence in the countries where they served as Peace Corps volunteers. Both Peace Corps staff and volunteers are limited to serving a maximum of five years at a time. They are allowed to reenter service only after they have spent the same amount of time out of the Peace Corps as the duration of their previous assignment. This rule has been established to keep the staff and volunteers fresh and innovative and to prevent volunteers and staff from turning the Peace Corps into a career.

Peace Corps/Nepal staff and volunteers

Peace Corps/Nepal

Peace Corps / Nepal started in 1962. One hundred volunteers served in the first group, in the fields of education and agriculture. Since then more than four thousand volunteers have served in Nepal in various programs, mainly education, health, agriculture, drinking water, fisheries, suspension bridge construction, and small-business development. Peace Corps/Nepal was forced to reduce the number of volunteers in the year 2000 due to budgetary constraints. After successfully serving for forty-two years, the program in Nepal was officially closed in September 2004, because of safety and security problems due to Maoist insurgents. After an eight-year gap, a group of twenty Peace Corps volunteers entered Nepal in 2012 to work in the fields of agriculture and nutrition. The Peace Corps programs continued to thrive all over Nepal and was well respected by the Nepali community. Then the deadly disease, coronavirus became a worldwide problem in 2020 and Peace Corps volunteers were brought back to the US not only from Nepal but from all over the world.

Peace Corps/Nepal staff, 1993. Left to right, back row: Dawa Thapa, Annie Martell, Lynn Poole, Renee Thakali. Middle row: Scott (Nepal desk officer, PC/W), George Monagan, Tika Karki, Tim Olmsted, Will Newman (country director). Front Row: B. L. Shrestha, Ambika Joshee, Dr. Madhu Ghimire, Shekhar Regmi, Shivaji Upadhyaya.

Joining the Peace Corps / Nepal staff

I joined the staff of Peace Corps/Nepal in 1971 as a language trainer and cultural informant. For the first two weeks, a group of new staff was trained in language teaching, and then we started teaching the Nepali language to the trainees from the day they landed in Nepal.

I then switched to working as an administrative assistant for the training program. It was an interesting job for me, as I had previously had very limited contact with non-Nepali speakers. My prior interactions with foreigners had been limited to my seven-week training seminar in Beirut, the two agriculture volunteers working in my cooperative office, and a few Peace Corps education volunteers in schools where I was teaching.

From my start with the Peace Corps as a language teacher, I became an administrative assistant. After that, a general services assistant and assistant program officer. In 1979, I became a program officer, specifically an associate Peace Corps director/education (APCD/Ed), a title I held until I retired from the Peace Corps in 2001. The next few chapters describe some of the cultural experiences I faced during these thirty years of service with Americans of all ages and backgrounds.

Peace Corps Director Carol Bellamy's visit to Nepal. From left: Renee Thakali, Dawa Thapa, Peace Corps Director Carol Bellamy, Tika Karki, and Ambika Joshee

Rum and Tequila

I had just completed my first assignment as a language trainer in a Peace Corps training program. I had worked with a few Peace Corps volunteers on an individual basis while I was working as district co-operative manager in Chitawan and also while teaching at Chitawan High School, but I did not have experience working as their tutor and cultural informant. It was an extremely good experience that I would not want to trade with anything. It was also an eye-opening experience for me, as I was able to look into another culture and compare it with my own. It was not easy to guess where the volunteers were coming from with their questions, decisions, and perceptions, which were, of course, based upon what they had seen and experienced back home in America.

Many times, they asked questions that were strange, irrelevant, and trivial from our point of view, such as "What is *jutho*?" "Why am I not allowed to eat in the kitchen with the family?" This happened especially in Brahmin families. "Why are others afraid to come close to us when we have our periods?" They asked me many questions for which I did not have easy answers.

My first training experience was in Kathmandu, followed by about two weeks in Dharan to experience the "homestay" phase of the training. In this phase, the volunteers stayed and ate both meals with the family. The plan was to expose them directly to Nepali life and culture. Some volunteers really enjoyed the homestays, while others had problems adjusting to life with their families. We, as cultural informants, spent a lot of time discussing issues with the trainees as well as their homestay families. The families needed as much help understanding the volunteers' behavior as a manifestation of American culture as the volunteers needed to understand the families' behavior as a manifestation of Nepali culture.

Many of the Nepali families had never seen or heard of cultures outside of Nepal. While there are cultural differences among the different tribes, castes, and ethnic groups of Nepal, they seldom question each other's way of life. Young Americans are brought up being encouraged to ask questions when they do not understand something. In Nepali culture, anything said by a senior person of the family is viewed as an unwritten rule and seldom questioned. Depending on the ethnic group, some taboos seem so strange to outsiders, and some of the unwritten rules are as if etched in stone. During this first Peace Corps training program, I had to explain many aspects of Nepali culture that I had never questioned myself.

After completing my assignment in the training program, I was on my way home from Kathmandu to Chitawan. I caught a ride in a Peace Corps vehicle going to Hetaunda. A program officer was visiting his volunteers there. When Peace Corps staff traveled in the field, it was customary to throw a small party for volunteers in the area. We planned a get-together that night in one of the volunteers' *dera* (apartment). There were about six or seven volunteers in the vicinity of Hetaunda Bazaar, and all of them were invited.

As I walked into the room, they had already started drinking. There were several bottles of rum and some other alcoholic beverages that I had not heard of before. I sat down in a corner and took some rum and wanted to mix in some water. In training we had access to the US commissary, where we could buy duty-free drinks and American comfort food, but we had no such facilities at a volunteers' post. After putting some water in my rum, I took a sip and found that it was still very strong. I kept adding water, but it felt stronger and stronger and tasted different each time I mixed more water in.

Finally, I came to a stage where I could not drink any more. I asked one of the volunteers why the taste was getting funnier and stronger. He asked me what I had been mixing in my rum. When I pointed out the bottle to him, he started laughing. Then, after a while, he explained to me that what looked like water was in fact a bottle of tequila. I had never heard of or seen tequila before. Then I came to know that it is a very famous drink in Mexico.

They also explained to me how they drink tequila, with a piece of lemon in one hand and a pinch of salt between the thumb and index finger of the other hand and a glass of tequila in the same hand. People lick the skin between the thumb and forefinger on the back of the hand before sprinkling a small pinch of salt. The moisture will help the salt stick on the skin. Then you lick the salt, take a shot of tequila, and bite or squeeze the lemon in your mouth. People often drink good tequila straight, but lower-quality tequila is often drunk with salt and lemon because of its harshness. It was a very new experience for me.

A Dream That Did Not Come True

Growing up in Bandipur and Narayanghat, I had seen poverty-related illness among the poor people of the area. Many people were unable to take care of their medical problems due to a lack of financial resources, which inspired me to think about going to medical school. I had that thought in my mind even after I joined Peace Corps, but deep inside, I knew it was not going to happen. The Peace Corps had already opened up many new avenues and new opportunities for me.

It was my first job as an administrative assistant for a training program. Before taking this position, I had worked as a language trainer in two other programs. The admin assistant position was more demanding and had taught me how to be more resourceful. I had to manage petty cash, medical issues, and relations with host families. The most demanding was handling and finding answers for medical-related questions. Finding answers to trainees' other questions was equally challenging. What we saw in our everyday life growing up in the villages did not seem like "everyday life" for these volunteers. Our upbringing was quite different. Seeing a rat running around the house did not make me scream, but I got questions like "I saw a rat in my room last night. Can I get rabies from rat bites?" I did not have answers to many of these questions, so I had to tell them to save these questions for the medical staff. Inside, I wished I had answers, I wished I had a medical degree to answer these questions, and I wished I had qualifications. Then I knew my desire for medical school and my curiosity and inclination toward health education was real.

These questions were a part of everyday debriefing. We had debriefing sessions every morning for half an hour before language classes. Breakfast was at seven in the morning, and the debriefing session followed right after. During every debriefing, the project director would start the session with an introduction, and then I ran the debriefing session to find out how each volunteer was doing. Debriefing sessions were full of questions. "I went to the kitchen to get my food last night, and all of a sudden I noticed that they had fed all the *dal bhat* to their cows. Did I do something wrong?" Or, "I told my *aamaa* (mom) that I was having my period, and she told me not to touch anything in the house and not to go near my brothers and my *baa* (dad). Why?" I did not have all the answers, and at times, I was not comfortable providing the answers. I asked the female language trainers to respond to female-related questions, but I had to field those questions myself most of the time. All the language, technical, and cross-cultural coordinators would sit in the debriefing session, but they were responsible only for the questions in their respective fields; the rest were mine. I knew where the questions were coming from. I could only imagine what it was like being in a different country with a different culture and language all at the same time. These trainees were brave and resourceful. They tried to find answers, but when introduced to a new culture and society, they were careful to follow the tradition and not disrespect. They needed answers and understanding and comfort to have a sense of belonging to their new "adopted" culture and society.

When I started working as a language trainer, I was unmarried. As I was from a lower-middle-class Newar family, I had to work while most of my friends enjoyed college life paid for by their families. I had dreams and ambitions for higher education. However, working full time while continuing my education was the only way for me to fulfill this dream. I knew at this point that my hope of going to medical school was an impossible dream. I did not have the opportunity to take loans or get financial help from family. I had heard of Peace Corps volunteers talking about their life in America. In America, after high school, students often go to college without depending on their family. They get loans for their studies, which they have to pay back after finishing school. This was not a possibility for me. Medical school had been one of my dreams when I was young, but life took a different direction, which, in retrospect, turned out to be a good direction.

Social and Cultural Taboos and Family Obstruction

Working at the Peace Corps, I came in close contact with volunteers, both male and female. Immediately after training, we had to escort volunteers to their posts and spend several days with them to make sure their living situation, food arrangements, teaching schedule, and other aspects of village life were settled and that the volunteers were comfortable while starting their new life.

After one of the trainings, I was assigned to take a female volunteer to her post in a remote village in eastern Nepal. This village was several hours' walk from the roadhead. After the volunteer finished all her shopping for food and other necessities, we left from Kathmandu. Our first stop was Narayanghat, a town where many faces and landmarks were familiar to me and brought back childhood memories. We stopped and had dinner with my family. Everyone at the house was curious. "Why is Ambika traveling with an American girl?" Before too many questions were asked, I explained that my job included traveling with the volunteers. But my mother was not satisfied. I could see on her face that she had questions. She was considerate enough to hide her feelings in front of the American guest, but she pulled me aside, saying "Stop by the house on your way back."

On my way back to Kathmandu, I made sure to stop in Narayanghat. My mother was waiting for me. She had not forgotten. She asked me the same questions again, and my answers were the same. But my mother was still not convinced, because in Nepali culture it is improper for an unmarried man to travel with an unmarried woman.

I left home at an early age. I was independent and had been making my own decisions for years. But my mother made me stop and think. She reminded me of our culture and our pride in being Nepali. She wanted my assurance that I was not bringing a foreign woman home. I was reminded to preserve my culture and follow what is "correct." I was told that a son's duty was to marry a Nepali woman of our caste, and only then could I perform my duty as a loyal family member. I would not be allowed to perform the last rites when she died if I married an American woman. Her words echoed again and again. It was not easy to listen to what she had to say. I was not planning to marry an American. In fact, I had no plan to get married anytime soon, but my mother's confident voice was enough for me to realize she meant what she said.

Tying the Nuptial Knot

I was looking for a permanent job and had been selected for a research officer position at the Agricultural Input Corporation (AIC). But I was attracted to the Peace Corps because my old friend Chij told me that I would have a chance to go to the Philippines as a language trainer if I started teaching immediately. Since my trip to Beirut in 1969, I had had a craving for international travel. I decided to work for the Peace Corps and gave up the more secure position with AIC. After I returned from the Philippines and completed my assignment to teach the Nepali language to Peace Corps trainees coming to Nepal, I had several successive personal service contract (PSC) jobs with the Peace Corps, working in training as a language instructor and later as an administrative assistant. I wanted to find the best position for myself in the Peace Corps and wanted to have a feel for the different jobs available at that time.

In one training program, I was assigned to a group that had intensive language training as well as a homestay program to be conducted in Dharan. This was where I met Kamala, my wife to be, for the first time. She had just come back from working in several training programs in Davis, California. She was working as a language coordinator in the program, and I was an administrative assistant. After this program there was another training program in Pokhara, where we worked together and got to know each other better. We started going on outings, we went to see Hindi movies, and we had lunch together regularly while in Pokhara.

I was surprised when Phyllis Hoffman, the Peace Corps administrative officer, visited the training site, she took time to interview me and then offered me my first permanent Peace Corps job, at the office in Kathmandu. I had no knowledge about this job opening, and I had not applied for it. But she somehow came to know about me from my performance in previous training programs. One week after that, I went to Kathmandu to sign my contract, expecting to start work after the completion of the training program.

After the end of the training in Bagar, Pokhara, another training was going to take place soon in Batulechaur, also in Pokhara. The training officer had not found another administrative assistant for this training program, so the training officer and administrative officer decided to let me work in the upcoming training program and postpone my job as general services assistant until the completion of this training.

It was the summer of 1972. I was busy at the training site in Pokhara. After about a week of orientation in Kathmandu, the trainees were driven to Pokhara for their three-month Pre-Service Training (PST). Training began with the first week of intensive language training, and each trainee was placed with a Nepali family.

As an administrative assistant, my regular duties included visiting trainees in their Nepali homes to find out about their living situation and their interactions with the family members. I especially wanted to know if the water was boiled and if the dishes and utensils were properly dried. We didn't want anyone to get sick. My other job included handling all training finances and logistics and finding families for the trainees' placement. I reported to the project director and prepared financial reports to send to the administrative officer in Kathmandu.

Language classes were scheduled in the morning. Language teachers would teach in the trainees' homestay villages. As a language coordinator, Kamala needed to go to the villages to observe language classes every day. As an administrative person, I also had to visit all these trainees and their Nepali families, so we usually planned our trips together. On these visits, I spent time with the Nepali families while she observed language classes and gave feedback to the teachers.

Born to a well-off family in Dhankuta, Kamala had taught English at Gokundeshwor High School for several years after completing her bachelor's degree. She had been to Kathmandu for TEFL (Teaching English as a Foreign Language) training at the British Council. Dorothee Goldman, one of the volunteers who was assigned to her school, saw her talent as a teacher and recommended her to the Peace Corps office. The Peace Corps selected her to go to the United States to teach Nepali.

Kamala's career in the Peace Corps started at the University of California Davis campus at Cactus Corners, where she taught the Nepali language for two years. In those days, all Peace Corps training took place in the United States, so language teachers were flown from Peace Corps countries to conduct training. All the Nepal Peace Corps training was held in Davis. Going to America was an unattainable dream for many people. People who had been to America were respected and considered somehow special. Kamala came back to Nepal around the end of 1970 and since then had been working in different Peace Corps training programs.

While working in the training program with her, I noticed Kamala's natural beauty, unadorned with makeup—which attracted many people, including me. Kamala is small in stature and overall, very charming. Language teachers respected her as a good supervisor; she provided critical feedback when needed, helping the language trainers hone their teaching skills. She also coached the language trainers in preparation of their lesson plans. After the morning rounds, we often went out for lunch together. Technical and cultural sessions were held in the afternoons, so we were usually free at those times except when Kamala had to help language trainers prepare their lesson plans. We usually ate lunch next to our training office at a small shop with *dal bhat* and other local foods like *selroti* and *pakauda*. I usually ate *dal bhat*, whereas I remember Kamala preferring a plate of *tarkari* (vegetables) and occasionally a selroti. This frequent lunching together and morning rounds to the villages became our regular routine in Pokhara and gave us a chance to know each other better, and we became close friends. Those two months flew by.

A few weeks before the completion of training, the trainees were given a ten-day break during which they were to go on a trek, make all their arrangements themselves, and report about their trek after the break. It was like an Outward Bound survival program in that they had to make do with their rudimentary knowledge of the Nepali language and culture—a test of how well they would be able to survive in the village. While the trainees were trekking, the staff decided to go to Kathmandu, as there was no work to be done for those ten days. Some people decided to drive back to Kathmandu, but I decided to fly the next day, as I had some last-minute work left to be completed. I tried to persuade Kamala to fly with me, but I was not successful. She decided to go with the rest of the group in a rental vehicle.

The day after I got to Kathmandu, I learned that the rental vehicle had had an accident immediately after leaving Mugling, where they had stopped for *dal bhat*. They managed to get help from the nearby military camp and were taken to Kathmandu. There were no casualties except that Kamala had a broken collarbone. I visited her quite often while she was on bed rest. After a week we returned to Pokhara, where I served as her health assistant, changing her bandages every day.

The swearing-in ceremony was held on the banks of the Kali river. As it was an education program, the district education officer, the chief district officer, and the district head of the police were invited, as well as the host families where volunteers had been posted for their homestay program. The American ambassador to Nepal at that time was on a trek in the surrounding hills, and she had agreed to swear in the trainees. She showed up in old jeans and dyed red hair. The Nepalis were curious about her appearance because she had been introduced as such an important person. Our program officer, Jeff Malik handled it very well, explaining that she had just come back from her trek and had not had time to go to her hotel and change. For some reason, the

Jeff Malik, program officer, swearing in volunteers

ambassador had to leave the site early and Jeff Malik ended up swearing in the volunteers.

Kamala was aware of my strong feelings for her, but I had no pressure from her to marry immediately. I had still not been able to express my love for her out loud. I don't remember exactly how and when it started, but I think our hearts were drawn closer to each other day by day, especially after that accident.

Even though we had not talked about getting married, I invited her to come with me and visit my family on our way to Chitawan while taking a volunteer to his post. I introduced her to my family members as my colleague from my work, but my mother and other family members read our minds. My family felt comfortable with her, but they were curious to find out more about her background, her family's status, and which subcaste of Newar they were. My mother was also trying to find if I was serious about my relationship with Kamala. But they had to wait until we got back to Kathmandu and shared our feelings.

Back in Kathmandu, I started my GSA role while Kamala kept her language-teaching job. We remained in close contact for the next year and remained good friends. Both of us were getting pressure from our respective families to get married. We also thought we should take the next step in our relationship. I informed my mother about our decision, and she came to Kathmandu to finalize our wedding. Kamala also informed her brother through her sister since in our culture the bride to be does not feel comfortable conveying the message directly to her family about her desire to marry a certain person as arranged marriage is still prevalent in Nepal to some extent. The bride to be usually finds somebody who can convey the message to the parents. Then the parents from both sides meet and arrange the wedding. Kamala's brother, Basanta Kumar Karmacharya, came with his nephew, Naresh, to my cousin's house, where I was living. My family asked Kamala's brother about their caste and other related questions. My brother-in-law was a lieutenant colonel in the Nepali army—we used to call him Colonel Bhinaju (older sister's husband) with respect, honor, and affection. He was posted in Dhankuta for several years, knew Kamala's family very well, and reassured my mother that they were well respected and of a similar caste to ours. The wedding plans were finalized that very night.

Our wedding: Kamala's sister Indu tying Kamala's maalaa (garland)

Our wedding took place in Budhanilkantha Temple, on the northern edge of Kathmandu Valley, with all our family members from both sides. A *purohit* (priest) conducted the ceremony with all the rituals, including the *hawan* (a rectangular fire pit where several kinds of grains mixed with *ghee* are tossed in the fire to please Hindu gods and goddesses). Each of us had a piece of cloth; these were tied together, and as we held on, the priest asked us to circle the hawan three times. We had two big parties. The first, before the wedding, was hosted by Kamala's family. And the one after the wedding was hosted by my family. Colonel Bhinaju was the happiest of all of us, and I still remember him dancing to the music provided by the army band he had arranged for the wedding.

At the wedding: Col. Bhinaju and Ambika

Colonel Bhinaju was my mentor in every sense during that stage of my life. Even though I was thirty years old, I was not careful about my finances. His first act to help me settle in Kathmandu was to have me open a bank account when I received my first paycheck in my new job with Peace Corps. He seemed to know that I was not going to go back to Chitawan after we got married. He wanted to help us buy a piece of land to build a house. With this idea in mind, it happened that he had already talked to some real estate agents and had found a suitable piece of land for us. When I told him that we didn't have enough money to buy land in Kathmandu, he gave me a blank check in my name. He said to draw as much money as we needed to buy this land and to pay him when we started saving from our earnings. The trust he had in me was unbelievable. We ended up not borrowing any money from him because Kamala and I managed to pay for the land from our savings. We had to wait several years to build our house.

My First Trip to the US

After working as a general services assistant (GSA) for four years, I became an assistant program officer, still in Peace Corps. Things were going well, but I was still not fully satisfied. I was looking for ways to climb my professional ladder. From GSA I could have been promoted to administrative officer, but until that time, only Americans had been considered for this position. On the program side, there were two American and three Nepali program officers with two Nepali secretaries. I thought I might have a chance at the program officer position. The program officers were having problems liaising with their Nepali counterparts at the government ministries, and I thought I could help them.

One day, Virgil Miedema, an American program officer, quietly asked me if I was interested in the program side. He told me they needed somebody who could work well with Nepali government officials. After I expressed my interest, he started talking to his colleagues, as well as the country director. After that I was transferred to the program side as an assistant program officer.

I worked as an assistant program officer for a year, assisting all five program officers. It was not easy to please five bosses. Going back and forth to different ministries was my main job. Whenever the program officers had any problem with the ministry officials, they sent me to the ministry to take care of it. In 1979, Virgil's two-and-a-half-year term was coming to an end, and the country director, Doug Pickett, promoted me to program officer. I think Virgil must have recommended that I be promoted, as he was impressed with how well I had learned my role as an assistant program officer. We had gone to the field together several times visiting current volunteers and checking sites for future volunteers' placement. After being promoted to program officer, APCD, I worked closely with Virgil for a few months, until his departure. It was helpful for me to overlap with him for those months, going out with him to visit volunteers and to do post surveys. I also worked with him on preparing volunteers' job descriptions and reports to be submitted to Peace Corps / Washington (PC/W). After Doug Pickett finished his term, Lynn Knauf replaced him. When I was promoted to program officer, Lynn arranged for me to take a trip to the United States for staff training, recruiting, and also to work in the Center for Assessment, Staging and Training (CAST). I also spent a few days at the Nepal desk office in Washington, DC, to familiarize myself with the team that dealt with volunteers' parents and other issues at home. Lynn had taken care of everything, including my flight details and travel advance, and had also told the Nepal desk officer in Washington that I was new to the job and had not been to the US and that I could use her help. My friends and colleagues also gave me an informal orientation to life in the US.

I took the Thai Airways flight from Kathmandu to Bangkok. After several hours' layover in Bangkok, I took a Pan Am (Pan American World Airways) flight from Bangkok to Dulles Airport in Washington, DC. The flight was fully booked, and it was long, but I enjoyed it. Our plane landed at Dulles the next afternoon. The Nepal desk officer, Christine Leggett, met me outside customs. I had no problem with immigration, as I was traveling under a US government business visa. The minute I collected my baggage and got into Christine's car, my dream visit started to unfold. Nothing was like what I had imagined.

The trip from the airport to the hotel was impressive. Christine drove me on a road with dense forest on both sides. We were driving on Route I-495, also known as the Beltway. The greenery on the highway was surprising to me at that time. It showed how much Americans value nature. Until then, I had assumed that the actual forests would have been cut down to build a concrete forest of high-rises, but I was wrong. Where these trees receded, the grasses and bushes were freshly manicured, with colorful flowers brightening the scenery. I was in awe of the deep blue sky, lack of stray animals on the road, and the complete absence of any littering or noise pollution as traffic moved smoothly on these highways.

Freshly painted white and yellow lines clearly marked the lanes of the road. It seemed so organized, with a low barrier in the middle of the road dividing traffic going in different directions and eight- to ten-foot walls to separate the residential areas from the Beltway. The green plantings made the roads look spectacular. I could not do anything but marvel at the highway system of the United States of America. It astonished me that even with the long lines of traffic on both sides of the road, sometimes bumper to bumper, people drove patiently without honking or yelling at each other. On highways, drivers adhered to the speed limit, which was clearly marked.

I often felt people were wasting their time and money waiting at a red light even when there was no vehicle or pedestrian coming from the other direction. In the same way, pedestrians waited for the Walk sign even when there were no vehicles on the road on any of the four sides. Maybe these are signs of civilization—citizens abiding by the rules, even with nobody watching to enforce the law.

The staff at the Peace Corps office was friendly and went out of their way to help me. I had a lot of questions about the US culture and specifically about Peace Corps work culture. Going to a restaurant and choosing food was challenging. When the person behind the register asked, "What do you want in your sandwich?" I had never heard of half of the ingredients that were available. Christine was patient with my curiosity. Most of the time she ordered my lunch.

One afternoon I bought my lunch from a fast-food place and went to a park close to the office to eat. While I was eating, a man in his forties came up to me and asked me if I was going to eat my bread. I could not make any sense of his question. Later on, one of my colleagues explained that he could have been a homeless man. I found out later that bread is usually free in restaurants when you order other food from the menu. I also noticed that people were feeding their bread to the pigeons in the park, and some were just throwing their bread into the trash. While there was clearly an abundance of food in this country, homelessness and hunger were still prevalent.

My first day at the office, Christine explained how to get to my hotel. It was just several blocks away from the office, not more than a fifteen- or twenty-minute walk, but she recommended that I take the metro. Later I found out that this is not considered walking distance for people here.

The Washington, DC, train system was also a surprise for me. The underground train in DC, called the metro, was new in the seventies. I could not believe how well organized the DC metro was. How can the machine figure out what distance you have traveled? How can it say "Add fare" if you don't have enough money on your fare card? Everything was so automated. It was not only me—I saw many US tourists confused at the metro station as well. I felt proud when I was able to explain how to use the metro after being there for a week or so.

The CAST was held at Harpers Ferry in West Virginia. It was a group of about thirty young people who wanted to be Peace Corps volunteers. CAST was a selection process involving Peace Corps staff as well as psychologists (nicknamed "shrinks"). I worked there as a resource person explaining the volunteers' work, the living situation, the lack of familiar foods and other essential materials, and communications in Nepal. This activity made the participants anxious, and some immediately deselected themselves. A few people who really wanted to go were not selected. They were upset, but there was nothing they could do. One person was nearly rejected but came to talk to me. After spending several hours with him, I was convinced that he could be a good volunteer. I lobbied with the CAST staff and got him selected.

I remember he completed his two years of service successfully and extended for a third year.

Briefing Peace Corps / Washington director Richard Celeste
about programs in Nepal.

I'm One Dollar Short for my Dinner

Back in DC, I took the metro from Farragut West to DuPont Circle after work, which was about a ten-minute walk to the friend's place where I was staying. I was still new in the area. I got off the train and took the escalator to the ground level, where an old lady, probably in her sixties, approached me, saying "I am one dollar short for my dinner. Could you help me, please?" She was nicely dressed and looked neat and clean. From our Nepali standards, I could never imagine that she was begging for a dollar. What a polite way of begging! Did she have a house to live in? What happened to her family? What happened to the government-supported Social Security system? Was she not eligible for food stamps? Some of these questions hit me hard in the context of what I had heard about this country. This one particular case left a strong impression in my mind.

I had seen people playing musical instruments and passersby dropping coins or dollar bills in a hat or their guitar case placed in front of them. But this lady astounded me. Hesitatingly, I put a dollar bill in her hand and looked at her for her reaction. She smiled and thanked me. I had just taken a few steps toward my apartment when I heard the same voice and same words. That made me believe that she was not just one dollar short, but that was a trick she used to get money.

I saw homeless people on the street. Some were not particularly old or disabled looking. These people would stand near intersections with cardboard signs reading "I'm a homeless man, please help me" or something like that. I saw them carrying all their belongings in a big plastic bag. By appearance, without my knowing their personal problems, if they had any, they looked perfectly capable of doing some kind of work to earn a living. I also saw many veterans on the streets who might have been suffering from post traumatic stress disorders (PTSD) and other mental illnesses. I can understand people begging if they can't work, but if people are physically and mentally fit, why should they not find some work to support themselves? A country with programs to help disabled individuals get proper jobs has able-looking people begging for help on the street corners! It was difficult to believe my eyes and ears. For me, it was surprising to see beggars on the road in the biggest economy of the world. Probably that was why the argument for more equal distribution of resources is gaining more ground in this country. Similarly, in Nepal, we experienced B. P. Koirala's attempt to initiate democratic socialism in Nepal, which was to have taken care of Nepal's inequalities.

The system is not perfect anywhere, and the representative democracy of the United States of America is not an exception. There are always drawbacks to each system. But in my first trip to the USA, these scenarios certainly puzzled me.

Red Wine with a Scoop of Sugar

After spending about a week at the Peace Corps office in Washington, we went on a recruiting trip to New York, Boston (called "Beantown" for their famous baked beans), Bangor, Augusta, and other cities in Maine. The whole New England trip was an eye opener for me. I flew from Dulles to JFK airport and took a train to Penn Station in New York as I had been advised by the staff in DC. I got out at Penn Station and went to a telephone booth to make a call to the New York recruiting office. I put in my quarters and dialed the number. The place was so noisy I could not make any sense of what the person on the other end of the line said, even though she repeated what she was saying two or three times. I just told her my name and told her that I would be at the office at 10:00 a.m. the next morning. I felt uneasy, even humiliated, for not being able to have a proper conversation with her. But I had no other way to communicate with her. The idea of what she might have thought of me came to my mind again and again. It was my first experience in New York. Welcome to the Big Apple.

In comparison to Washington, DC, New York was very crowded. The skyscrapers were unbelievably tall, and traffic was crazy. Also, New York was not as clean as Washington. The vast number of pedestrians also surprised me. It reminded me of Indrachowk and Ason Tole in Kathmandu.

A friend's parents had graciously invited me to stay with them while I was in New York. My friend in Nepal had sent them a message telling them that I was visiting the US and might come to New York sometime, so they had contacted Peace Corps office in DC and requested my travel schedule. When they found out about my arrival to New York, they called to assure me I could stay with them. Although many Americans often go out to eat, my hosts prepared meals at home according to my taste. They were nice people who made me feel like I was at home immediately after I met them.

The next day I had to go to the New York recruiting office, so my hosts drove me to the subway station. They told me to be careful at the subway station. At that time I did not know why I needed that warning, but later on I found out mugging and other crimes are rampant in New York, especially in and around certain neighborhoods. I saw a lot of graffiti on the walls, which I had not noticed in Washington. I noticed many differences between these two cities.

My third day in New York, I was invited by a RPCV for a reception. He had recently married a Nepali girl, who happened to be on the same plane as I was from Kathmandu to Bangkok. In Bangkok she had told me that she was going to New York to teach the Nepali language to Peace Corps volunteers, which had surprised me because I knew there was no such Peace Corps program in New York. In New York I found out that she had been traveling to meet her fiancé, whom she married just after her arrival.

I went to this reception and met the RPCV, John, and his Nepali wife, Karuna. She could not believe it when she saw me there. Even though John had told her that one of his Nepali friends was coming to the reception, she was not expecting to see me. I think she had not told her husband about our meeting at the Bangkok airport. As John had recently returned from Nepal, he and Karuna were living with his parents, and the reception was held at his parents' house. John's mother and I talked for a few minutes, and she pointed me to the refrigerator and told me to help myself to drinks. Karuna had been there for some time by then. When I went to the refrigerator to get a drink, Karuna came to help me. I told her I wanted some iced tea with a little bit of sugar. There were two similar bottles, neither with a label. The content of the bottles also looked the same color. Karuna poured me a glass from one bottle, which she said was iced tea. I added some sugar and went to the living room. It had a funny taste. It tasted like some kind of alcohol, but very sweet. After tasting it, I asked Karuna what it was, just to make sure. But she again told me that it was ice tea. When I had my second sip, Mrs. Hampton saw my puzzled face and asked me what I was drinking. I told her I had some ice tea with sugar. She took the glass from my hand and took a sip. She obviously didn't understand our concept of jutho, where we don't eat from the same plate or drink from the same glass as others. She must have realized what had happened, because she asked me which bottle my drink came from. When I pointed to the bottle, she told me that it was some sort of wine that she had brewed herself at home. She immediately threw that sugared wine in the sink and gave me some iced tea with sugar in a new glass.

After a few days in New York, I went to Boston and met with the recruiter who was to join me for the trip through Massachusetts and Maine. We covered a large part of New England. We did a series of recruiting sessions in Massachusetts and Maine, some in hotels and some on university and college campuses.

In Bangor, Maine, I was interviewed live on local TV for about half an hour. It was my first live appearance on TV, and I was very nervous, but I had a seasoned reporter who started by asking simple questions about Nepal, slowly leading me into the main topic of Peace Corps and our recruiting trip. By the middle of the interview, I was relaxed, and the interview went very smoothly. Overall, it was a good recruitment trip, and my work was appreciated at Peace Corps headquarters and especially at the recruitment office in Boston.

After I returned to Washington, DC, the staff asked me about my impressions of America—what I liked the most and the least. I remember one particular conversation when a colleague asked, "What do you think about American society? Tell me something positive and something negative." The positive feeling was not a problem. I had a lot of them: clean environment, friendliness, ability to drink water straight from the tap, law-abiding citizens, and many more examples.

When I thought about the negative aspects, the first thing that came to mind was "It is a throwaway society." I remember a scene in a college cafeteria. Students would take as much food as they wanted, even when they knew they would not be able to eat one-quarter of the food they had taken. They would just eat a piece or two and dump the rest in the trash. This was hard for me to see, especially as I remembered the starving children in far western Nepal.

Another example that came to mind was the culture of throwing away equipment and gadgets if they had minor problems or when a newer version became available. One simple example is a cigarette lighter. In Nepal, people refill cigarette lighters ten to twenty times before they are discarded, while there is no concept of refilling in the US. I also saw people putting their old TVs, furniture, and other items out in the garbage. Sometimes I saw the neighbors picking them up, while most of the time they probably ended up in landfills. I even saw a garbage collector keeping an item for himself.

In Bangor, the Peace Corps had made a reservation for me in a hotel with breakfast included. Even though it was summertime, Bangor was a little chilly. I was busy for the whole day with my recruiting duties at hotels and college campuses. After the day's activities, I went back to my hotel, ate, and went to bed. The next day I had to leave the hotel around nine o'clock to start my journey back to Boston. I wanted to have breakfast before my departure. I went to the dining hall and looked at the menu for breakfast. I wanted to have something different and something that local people ate. So I ordered "farmer's pancakes." I was surprised when my order came. There were two huge pancakes about seven inches in diameter with a mound of whipped cream and several toppings including blueberries, which made it probably six inches high. Definitely not the healthy and wholesome breakfast that I had expected by the name "farmer's pancakes." I liked the taste, but I could not eat even half of the pancakes. I made my contribution to the "throwaway" culture of America. I would have taken it in a doggy bag if I were not traveling back to Boston, which was a full day's drive.

The Lady with an Elephant's Memory

Information technology was in its infancy. All the communication in the Peace Corps used to be with pen and paper. Email was not available, and the only way we could communicate quickly with Washington, DC was through the US embassy cable system. We used this system only for emergency or urgent matters. Otherwise, we communicated with everyone via letters. All communication was filed for future reference.

We had two filing systems in use in our office. All communications with volunteers were put in the volunteer's file, arranged alphabetically in file cabinets in the program offices. We also had chronological ("chron") files in the director's secretary's office. One of the file cabinets in the director's secretary's office contained separate copies of all the files for each month. Whenever we needed to find some information not in our office, we would go to the director's secretary's office to look in the chron file, which had all the communications of the whole office.

One day, I was looking for a letter that we had written to the Ministry of Education regarding house rent money for education volunteers. My secretary and I looked through all the files in our office but could not find the letter. I thought it was the month of September when I wrote that letter, but I could not remember the exact date. We decided to go to the director's secretary's office to look. Three of us (my secretary, the director's secretary, and I) were looking through the files when Lynn Knauf, our director, walked into the office. She asked us what we were looking for. I explained, and without any hesitation she said, "Look in the September file. It must be September 15." Lo and behold, there it was in the September file, and the date was September 15. Because of her sharp memory, she was known among the support staff as "the lady with an elephant's memory."

The Unsigned Divorce Papers

It was August 1982. Family life was going well. By this time, our daughter Jharana was six years old and Archana four. We had met an American architect who agreed to design a house for us near Ratopul in Kathmandu, on the property that Colonel Bhinaju had selected for us. After we explained our needs, the architect brought several cardboard models and asked us to select from them. Each one was different and a departure from anything found in Nepal at that time. What we chose was a unique design that the architect described as "a village in a house" because of the roof ending in three points, looking like several houses instead of one. Others think it looks like a temple.

Drawing of our house

We had two construction engineers to oversee the construction work, one Nepali and one British. I started the construction work thinking to have all Nepali laborers, but I ended up with almost exclusively Indian laborers, as I could not deal with the Nepalis' lax attitude: "be merry and enjoy as much as you can when you have some money in your pocket." Sometimes the Nepali laborers did not show up for work for days, without giving any notice, whereas the Indians were prompt and did not mind working overtime for a few extra rupees. This was probably because of the tight job market in India.

Immediately after our marriage, Kamala and I decided that we should not be working in the same office. Both of us agreed that there could be a conflict of interest in our work as well as the question of ethics. We were lucky that Ann Sturley, Kamala's friend—and also one of the editors of this book—was the academic director for the Nepal Semester Abroad Program of the School for International Training (SIT) headquartered in Brattleboro, Vermont. She told Kamala about the job of language coordinator and assistant to the academic director in SIT. Kamala applied and was offered the job. Both of our jobs involved a lot of field trips, but we were lucky in that I was able to plan my field trips so as to avoid conflict with her trips, which would happen at the beginning of the fall and spring semesters each year. House construction work was going well, although I had to work as an interpreter between five different languages: Nepali, Hindi, Bhojpuri, Newari, and English. We had American architects, British and Nepali construction engineers, Newari bricklayers, Bhojpuri-speaking rebar workers, and various Nepali- and Hindi-speaking laborers. I would sit down with these people every evening after I came home from work.

One afternoon, a volunteer showed up in my office without prior notice. Volunteers were required to have absence-from-post forms signed by their headmaster, who was their local supervisor, but this volunteer did not have that form. I asked him what was going on. He complained that his colleagues did not teach their full class period and that his headmaster was not a good administrator. This volunteer had come to Kathmandu without his headmaster's approval so he could discuss these issues with me. Part of my job was to mediate between the volunteers and locals of the area such as the headmaster, colleagues, house owners, and others. The volunteer was hesitant to go back to his village, but he agreed to go back if I went with him. I planned a four-day field trip starting the next day. A lot of work was going on at the construction site. Kamala was upset with this unplanned field trip coming out of nowhere.

The next day I left for four days. I visited the school and met the headmaster and other teachers. We had a long discussion about education administration, particularly as it related to that school. We also discussed teaching philosophy and how student-centered teaching can benefit the students. Finally, we came to the agreement that the teachers should be in the classrooms until the bell rings, that the headmaster is the person responsible for school administration, and that this volunteer also needed to respect the decisions of the headmaster. We also discussed the benefits of lesson plans and that each teacher should take the initiative to make lesson plans for every class they teach. The volunteer was happy, and I returned to Kathmandu the next day. Kamala was happy I was home—but the happiness remained only for a few days.

Sometimes Peace Corps emergencies occurred after office hours or on weekends. After-hours duty rotated among the five associate directors, the country director, the deputy country director, and the administrative officer. The week after I came back from that unplanned field trip, I happened to be on duty. The duty officer had to carry a beeper with him or her 24-7 so that the marine from the US embassy could contact him in case of emergency. That day around 2:00 p.m., I got a call from the marine informing me that a volunteer in the far western region had a medical emergency. I located the medical officer and the country director and discussed the issue.

We had engineers, laborers, and others preparing to pour the concrete for the roof of our building that day. Work was going at the new house as planned when I got that call from the marine. I instructed the engineers to continue the work in my absence and have it completed by the end of the day, as the pouring of the concrete for the floor had to be done the same day to avoid leakage and cracks. If the work did not get completed the same day, the concrete might not seal properly, and there could be leakage in heavy monsoon rains.

The medical officer was afraid that the volunteer could have a life-threatening situation and we would have to evacuate him. That meant I had to charter a helicopter and fly out there with a nurse. I went home and picked up my backpack, which I kept packed and ready, and explained the situation to Kamala. She was already upset with me about my last unplanned trip. On top of that, Jharana had a high fever and Kamala was busy taking care of her and was unable to go to work. Seeing me picking up my backpack and leaving, she burst into tears and said, "You are not married to me. You are married to your job and your volunteers. You don't care about our children and the work on the construction-site. You go do your job, and I will have the divorce papers ready, and you will just have to sign them after you come back from your trip."

I did not know what to do. I tried to talk to Kamala, but she did not want to listen to me. The vehicle was waiting to take me to the airport, and the helicopter was waiting for me at the airport. I came back home late that evening after dropping the volunteer at the medical office. The medical office was ready, as they knew a sick volunteer was arriving. Luckily, the volunteer got well and returned to his post in a few days.

When I got home, Kamala was still upset. I wanted to start our conversation with a joke and asked her where the divorce papers were. She laughed at me. I knew she has a kind nature. And luckily, I never had to sign those papers.

We had different personalities, which brought us closer. I had interest in politics and world news, whereas she was and still is more of a to-do point person on our own personal life issues rather than taking interest in politics and other matters. The ambivalence and decisiveness, depending upon the subject matter on the table; tolerance; and her farsightedness for the betterment of the family are some of the ingredients of the chemistry for the success of our family.

Crossing the Indian Border

The East-West Highway had not been built farther west than Butwal. People traveling from Kathmandu to the far western or midwestern regions of Nepal had no choice but to go via India. Our next trip was to visit volunteers in the Baitadi, Dadeldhura, Doti, and Bajhang districts. Visiting volunteers was a hectic and time-consuming task but one of the most important and most rewarding duties of the program officers. Visiting them was the best way to support them, to learn about their adjustment to village life, and for me, the best way to monitor the math and science education program. Input from volunteer visits played a vital role in the evaluation and monitoring of the entire Peace Corps / Nepal program and decisions for its continuity.

Sometimes it took eight to ten days just to visit one volunteer, primarily due to the amount of walking involved. We might fly to the closest airport and walk from there or drive to the roadhead and walk from there. Our plan was to drive to Bhairahawa and cross the Nepal-India border in Sunauli, drive from there all the way to Jhulaghat, and cross the India-Nepal border again in Jhulaghat to go to Baitadi.

Kathmandu to Bhairahawa was a long day's drive. The road was narrow and winding with many steep inclines. We decided to stay in the chamber of commerce guesthouse in Butwal that night. There were no good hotels those days, so we usually had to find a good guesthouse. The office helper at the guesthouse made good food, *chapatti* and *dal* and some vegetables for us. We were tired, so we ate and slept immediately, as we had a long day's drive the next day.

My colleague on this trip was Virgil Miedema, whom I previously mentioned as my guru who taught me many mantras for supporting volunteers and running the program. Sunauli had an immigration check post, but we did not have a problem crossing the border. We crossed early in the morning and ate our morning meal in Lukhnow.

We aimed to reach Pithauragarh that night, as we had to get a border-crossing permit for our American colleague from the magistrate of the Pithauragarh district. Our driver was an experienced ex-Indian army driver who had been working for the Peace Corps for the last ten years. The Indian roads looked much better than our roads in Nepal. This road was wide and well maintained. Premonsoon rains had just hit the area, so there was plenty of water for the farmers to prepare their fields for rice planting. Farmers were busy plowing the land and preparing to transplant rice. In comparison to our dry *tarai* flatlands, India had good irrigation systems, and their average harvest was much better than ours. About 95 percent of both the electricity and water for irrigation from the Koshi and Gandak dams goes to India. This clearly shows how Indian interests have taken precedence over Nepali interests in the treaties regulating these dams. Any visit to the border areas shows the heavy-handed activities of our big brother India. Still, the scenery was beautiful, with rivers swollen with monsoon rain, and the trees on the sides of the road had new bright-green leaves. Sometimes the Indian government kept the dam gates closed, flooding Nepali farms upstream.

We had about fifty education volunteers in Nepal in those days, and we were supposed to visit each of them at least once a year. We had to make several trips to visit any volunteer who had problems. Visiting fifty volunteers was not an easy task with the poor roads, and it took a lot of time away from my office work. As I had just started my job, I was still learning the ropes. This trip was my first and Virgil wanted me to pick up some of the many unwritten techniques for dealing with the volunteers and various situations. Virgil explained that our aim should be to see how they were doing in their work and in the village. We might have to mediate between the headmaster and the volunteer or the volunteer and his/her colleagues or even between the volunteer and his/her students or the villagers. Diplomacy was the key to success in this job. We also had to ascertain that the volunteers were doing their jobs properly and provide them with assistance in their technical field if needed. Program officers had to wear several different hats at a time—cultural, technical, and language expert—according to the needs of the situation.

We were responsible for helping them in all aspects of their life in the village. In the case of education volunteers, technical assistance meant helping them learn how to teach in a village school without any teaching aids and with only rudimentary Nepali language. Culture was another challenge. Yes, they had three months of intensive training in culture, language, and the technical aspects of teaching, but that was in no way enough to prepare them for village life in Nepal. In spite of the challenges, most of the volunteers were successful in accomplishing the three goals of the Peace Corps: Technical skill transfer, teaching Nepali people about America, and, hopefully, they would accomplish their third goal of teaching American people about Nepal after they returned home.

When we reached the magistrate's office in Pithauragarh, he was not there, so we met with the deputy magistrate. He was friendly and helpful at first. After we explained who we were and why we needed to cross the border at Jhulaghat, he told us that due to Sino-Indian border problems, we would not be able to cross the border there. India and China were having border problems at that time, and both countries had accumulated a large number of army personnel on the border. We told him that we had talked to the Indian ambassador to Nepal in Kathmandu, who had assured us that there should be no problem crossing the Jhulaghat border. Unfortunately, we had not brought a letter from the Indian ambassador. Having no letters from the embassy probably made him suspicious, as there were rumors of American government officials in Nepal and India being Center Intelligence Agency

(CIA) agents.

Finally, he told us that he would call the police officer in Jhulaghat and tell him to let us cross the border. We were pleased and thanked him and left his office. We knew that Indians and Nepalese had to get permits and foreigners were not allowed to cross the border at Dharchula which is a bordering town in India. We decided to go the Jhulaghat route. If not, the Dharchula route would have been much closer for visiting volunteers in Darchula, the district of Nepal.

We found a small hotel in Pithauragarh, where we spent the night. There were a lot of Nepalese working in the Pithauragarh area. Even though they spoke Nepali, we had a hard time understanding their language, as they spoke in the Baitadali dialect. Most of their verb endings and nouns sounded like Hindi. These were people from the far-western hill region of Nepal, mostly from Darchula, Baitadi, Bajhang and Achham, working as porters and doing other manual work there.

The next day we started our journey early in the morning. After reaching Jhulaghat, we went directly to the police office. On our way there, we had noticed an Indian government police jeep following us. When we reached the police office, we noticed that the Indian police jeep was parked in front of the police office. I didn't notice when and where he had overtaken us. After we went to talk to the police officer, two police personnel spent more than an hour opening all our bags, including volunteers' mail packages. Later, the police officer who had followed us from Pithauragarh told us that he had strict orders from the deputy magistrate to not let us cross the border in Jhulaghat. He told us that because of the Sino-Indian border dispute, the Indian central government had directed them to keep careful watch on all foreigners who were traveling in that part of the country. He initially told us to go back and cross the border where there was an immigration check post. But after a long discussion, we were finally able to convince the police officer. He called the Pithauragarh office and told them in detail about our luggage and finally got permission to let us cross the border. Even then, he was not very helpful, and we could not figure out the reason.

At the same time, our driver was talking to one of the junior police officers. The two of them had been discussing an issue for a long time, but we had no clue what was going on. After a while, our driver came to me and said he would like to talk to me alone. The driver and I went to a tea shop, and there he told me that the Indian police officer wanted some money. He explained that they had permission from Pithauragarh, but even then, they would not let us go if we didn't pay them. After a long a hassle, finally I was able to convince the Indian police officer that he was not going to get any money from us, as we were on an official trip and we could not bribe for our work.

We crossed the border. The walk from Jhulaghat to Gothalapani (the district headquarters) is about a two-hour walk, but it took us longer, as our backpacks were heavier than usual. Our driver went back to Kathmandu after making sure we successfully crossed the border, waiting until he saw us across the Mahakali River, climbing uphill toward Gothalapani.

Mohawk Hairstyle

The medical office had informed me that John Robinson needed to come to Kathmandu for medical reasons. Medical confidentiality was a big issue in Peace Corps, and we were not supposed to question the medical office about a volunteer's medical issues.

I got a call from the medical office on that Thursday afternoon saying that John had been released from medical hold, and now he could go back to his village in Chitawan. Early Friday morning John walked into my office to say that he was ready to go. I was in deep concentration on a phone conversation with another volunteer, so John had to wait for a few minutes. When I finally looked up, I could not believe my eyes. His hairstyle was something I had never seen before. He had cleanly shaved both sides of his head above his ears, leaving a swath of longer hair in the middle, all the way from his forehead to his neck. He had waxed his hair, and the hair was standing straight up. I was shocked and couldn't say anything. Finally, I broke the silence and asked him about his haircut. He explained to me that the style was called a Mohawk, after a Native American tribe who wore a similar style. John did not show any reaction to my surprise at his haircut. He took it very casually. But I was thinking about the teachers' and students' possible reaction at his school.

Then I asked him about the Mohawk hairstyle and if teachers in America went to school with this hairstyle. What about other professionals in America? He kept quiet for a while and told me that he had not seen any teacher with this hairstyle in an American school. He said that it was a fashion among young Americans but that people would not wear this haircut while working in a professional role. Then I asked him what made him think that it would be acceptable in a Nepali school. "I am a volunteer, and I should be allowed to wear my hair as I please" he responded. I reminded him that he was in Nepal by invitation from the government of Nepal. I told him that teachers had a special place in Nepali society. They were looked upon as a role model for the students. We had a long discussion about culture, the role of the teachers, and the teacher as a role model in the school and in the community. I was able to convince him that if that hairstyle was not appropriate for American schoolteachers, it was not appropriate for Nepali schools either. He agreed that he did not want to lose the respect he had garnered from his colleagues, his headmaster, and his students.

Our agreement was that he would shave his head before leaving for Chitawan and that he would wear a Nepali *topi* (cap) for at least three to four weeks while at school. I was glad it ended on a positive note and that John understood my concerns. Cultural sensitivity is a necessary path to acceptance by people of any culture. The Peace Corps idea of living in the village, eating with the family, following local rituals, and accepting local norms helps volunteers get immersed in village life, which also makes their life easier and more fulfilling. I know it is difficult for volunteers, coming from a country placing a high value on individual liberty and an open society, to adjust in a place where ancient traditional practices are still common and carry heavy weight. There is a delicate balance between acting on one's individual liberty and respecting the local norms.

Cultural differences are not a problem if each side is respectful of the other.

Connection

It was the summer of 1992. All education volunteers were in Kathmandu for summer conferences. It is customary for program officers to invite their volunteers for dinner or for a reception while they are in Kathmandu. This was always appreciated by the volunteers. Lack of comfort food was a big problem for many volunteers. Most of them had to eat the traditional Nepali *dal bhat* and *saag* at every meal. Sometimes I myself wondered how these people from a country of multiple choices and abundance survived here for two years while they struggled to adjust to the food, culture, and poor living standards in Nepal. Their experiences exposed them to the real life of people of a third-world country. Usually program officers would take nonperishable food like coffee, peanut butter, jam, granola, muesli, fruit, and chocolate bars when they visited volunteers. Some volunteers even received a "nutrition allowance" when they experienced too much weight loss. Volunteers filled their backpacks with food items while going back to post from Kathmandu. It was expected that the volunteers would have a good big meal at the program officer's residence in the summer when they came to Kathmandu for conferences.

That year, our elder daughter, Jharana, was working hard for her SLC examination. Jharana and Archana were attending St. Mary's High School in Jawalakhel, an English-medium Catholic girls' school. Both of them were doing well in their classes. Whenever I tried to help my daughters with their homework, they wanted me to use the exact same words that their teachers had used in the classroom, as the teachers emphasized rote memorization rather than meaningful learning. Meaningful learning allows students to be fully engaged in the learning process. It encourages students to actively participate in the learning process rather than just memorizing a book or lesson. Meaningful learning encourages students to think and understand the issues. In

Nepali schools the teaching styles were usually teacher centered rather than student centered. I even went to see one of their teachers to complain about this. The teacher's response was "How do you expect your teenage daughter to think for herself? The only way they can pass their SLC exam is by memorizing." I thanked her for her time and left our meeting because I realized I was not in a position to influence her teaching style.

Working in a Nepali high school as a headmaster for about ten years and working in the field of education in the Peace Corps for several years, I was very much aware of what went on in Nepali classrooms, which did not make me happy. I still think the Nepali education system needs an overall change to accommodate new scientific methods of classroom teaching. Critical thinking and questioning are not encouraged in our education system. Students are not encouraged to question; instead questioning is discouraged. "The nail that sticks out gets hammered." The government of Nepal has been working with the help of foreign donors to train Nepali teachers, but success has been minimal.

Education Peace Corps volunteers did classroom teaching in their first year to gain firsthand knowledge of the Nepali classroom. They then conducted teacher training in their second year in coordination with government-run primary and secondary teacher training projects.

Getting frustrated with the prevailing Nepali education system, we were looking for a way to provide a good education for our daughters. Our goal was to make them creative and independent. The teaching methods in Nepali colleges were similar to the methods that were in use in high schools. Professors prepared notes, recited these notes in class, and asked their students to memorize the notes, which were used year after year. Some professors just read from text books and elaborated a little bit—that was all that went on in Nepali classrooms. I had heard that Budhanilkantha school was a little better, but they had not started enrolling girls in their classes preparing for the British A-level and O-level exams, or grades eleven and twelve. I came to the conclusion that the only way to provide my daughters with a good education was to send them abroad.

That evening we had invited about fourteen or fifteen volunteers for dinner. We were having drinks before dinner, and one of the volunteers asked me about my plan for our daughters' education. All of them were education volunteers, teaching mathematics, science, and English in Nepali high schools, so they were aware of what went on in the classrooms in Nepal. The volunteers had fought with their colleagues, headmasters, and students in order to introduce new teaching methods in their classrooms. The volunteers wanted not only to change the teaching style but also to ban corporal punishment, but without much success.

I had been writing to private and charter schools in America, inquiring about the possibility of sending Jharana there for grades eleven and twelve. I chose private schools because I had heard that some private schools looked for bright students outside the US for a cultural exchange that would benefit both the foreign student and the local students. I also knew that some schools in America had student exchange programs. When the volunteers asked me about my plan, I shared my list of schools where I had sent application letters. The volunteers discussed how they could help me. They also talked about their links with different schools in America.

A quiet voice came from the corner of the room saying, "My son teaches in a private school, but he is just a teacher, and he would not have any say in decision-making." That was one of the volunteers, Edith Conzett. She was always polite and respected other people's thoughts and ideas. I had never heard her speaking in a loud voice. Edith was posted in Purbanchal Gyan Chakchhu Vidyalaya (school for the blind) in Dharan, where she was teaching braille.

Edith said she would write to her son and find out if there was any chance my daughter could attend his school. I shared my fear that private schools in America must be very expensive, and I would not be able to bear the burden of tuition and living expenses in the US. I was very impressed by the enthusiasm and concern that she and the other volunteers expressed that evening.

I had already received responses from some of the schools that I had written for information. They were very interested, but tuition and living arrangements were problematic. Some schools were willing to wave the tuition and other fees, but food and housing would have to be arranged, as they did not have hostels. Some schools sent long letters with detailed information, and some schools even called me to tell me that they would love to have our daughters if we could manage their living situation. The discussion with the volunteers had ended on a positive note. I was not expecting anything, and I had not said anything to my daughter. I did not want her to be expecting something that might not happen.

The volunteers' conferences were coming to an end. The volunteers had their own plans for the rest of the summer. Some had vacation plans, as their schools were closed for summer, and some were preparing to go back to their villages. Volunteers were allowed to take off from school only during vacation time as scheduled in the school calendar. Other than that, they could only take time off for medical reasons, for which they had to obtain an absence-from-post request approved by the medical office.

Edith had gone back to her post. About three weeks later, I got a call from her saying that her son, Peter Conzett, wanted me to fill out the application form he had just mailed to me, for acceptance to Falmouth Academy. Edith repeated that her son was just a teacher and couldn't promise anything. I was encouraged and hopeful for the first time. When the application forms arrived, I completed them very carefully and mailed them. There was no email in those days, as information technology was not as developed. It used to take ten to fifteen days for a letter from the US to reach Nepal. I told Jharana about the application but told her that the chances were very slim.

About a month later, I got a letter from Bruce Buxton, headmaster of Falmouth Academy, saying that he had accepted Jharana in grade eleven for the school session starting at the end of August. I could not believe it! I had heard from other schools that Jharana would have to pass the Secondary School Aptitude Test (SSAT) and the Test of English as a Foreign Language (TOEFL), and she had not taken either of these tests. I wrote back to Bruce, and he responded that he had used his authority to waive both of the tests and the tuition fee as the headmaster of the school.

Now we had to plan the trip. We happened to be very lucky. Peace Corps Washington had planned a CAST for new volunteer trainees around the middle of August, again in Harpers Ferry, where I had been on the last trip. I talked to Will Newman, Nepal country director, about Jharana's acceptance at Falmouth Academy and told him that I would like to take two weeks off from work to take Jharana to the US. He happily nominated me to participate in the conference, and I was invited to work at the Washington office for about ten days before the conference. Kamala had already prepared to participate in an orientation program at the SIT office in Brattleboro, Vermont, around the same time. Everything worked out perfectly for us.

Now I had to work on my travel plans, so I went and talked to Will Newman again. From earlier discussions he knew about Jharana's acceptance at Falmouth and my upcoming participation in CAST, so I requested one week of annual leave to go to Falmouth with Jharana to help arrange her living situation and also to meet with the school's faculty members. Will was happy with the arrangements and promised to do his best to help me. Since this involved international travel, Will needed approval for my leave from his boss, the regional director. He sent several cables requesting my leave, but he was not getting a positive response. He decided to call the Washington office late one afternoon.

That evening, as I was walking to his office, I heard him yelling over the phone, "Dammit, he is not going to lie on the beach. He is taking his daughter to school halfway around the world." Immediately I knew what he was talking about and who he was talking to. Later he told me that somehow he had convinced the regional director to approve my leave. This was Kamala's third trip to the US, my second, and Jharana's first. Jharana was very excited.

Before we left Nepal, Jean Mead, my Peace Corps counterpart who was taking care of the English education program, offered to spend some time with Jharana to talk about American culture. She would be a new foreign student in a school consisting of all American students. She thought Jharana needed to hear from a person who knew well the culture of schools in America, including which subjects are taught in which grades, boy-girl relations, and family life in America. We were very appreciative of Jean's spending time with Jharana.

Mark Nachtrieb (Nepal RPCV) was the CAST coordinator, and he had arranged a suite in a hotel in Washington, DC, as he knew that I was coming with my wife and daughter. We had a small kitchenette and were eating most of our meals at the hotel. One morning I tried to boil eggs for breakfast, and I put them directly in the microwave. I was surprised when I heard the sound of the eggs exploding. I did not know that I could not boil eggs in a microwave. First experience.

After a few days in Washington, we went to Falmouth to see the school and meet the faculty. We had to go to Union Station to get a bus to Falmouth. Until that time I did not know that there are some risky areas in DC. When people found out that we had taken a bus to Union Station, they told me they were glad we did not have a bad experience.

It was our first trip to Falmouth. We took a Greyhound bus for the first time in our lives. This bus and the ride itself were very different from what we were used to in Nepal. We met Mary Sellers (Jharana's host mother), Peter Conzett (Edith's son, math and physics teacher), Bruce Buxton (headmaster), and others in Falmouth. People had questions and were very interested to learn about Nepal and especially about Jharana, their student-to-be. Mary asked me a question that touched my heart and made me realize that I was leaving my vulnerable and impressionable teenage daughter in somebody's care for one whole year. She asked, "How do I deal with Jharana if she comes home late from a party or other gathering?" I had not contemplated that kind of a situation. Then I realized that Jharana was going to be in a new culture where it would not take much time to learn bad habits if she happened to be with the wrong company. Mary had a daughter who was a few years younger than Jharana. I asked her to do exactly what she would do with her own daughter. She was happy with my answer. I think we built trust between us with that conversation.

After a few days in Falmouth, we returned to DC, where I was busy with my work at the Peace Corps office. Kamala went to Brattleboro, Vermont, and then directly to Nepal. Jharana joined me for a week in Harper's Ferry in West Virginia and came back to DC with me. Melanie Landau, one of Kamala's friends, had been a Peace Corps Volunteer in Nepal and was teaching in a school in DC. She invited Jharana to visit her eleventh-grade math class. Jharana came back to the hotel excited to share her experience with us. She said that in tenth grade she had already mastered the math Melanie was teaching. We figured out that American history and writing classes would be more difficult for her. I bought some American history books and studied at night to help Jharana for her upcoming classes.

We returned to Falmouth. We spent some time with the headmaster, the school faculty, and Ms. Mary Sellers. The morning I was leaving Falmouth, as usual I woke up early. I took a quick shower and sat down with a cup of coffee, waiting for Peter Conzett. Peter had offered me a ride to Boston airport. While waiting for him, I was thinking about leaving Jharana without saying goodbye that morning. It was a mind-boggling situation. I was nervous. I knew it would not be an easy goodbye if I woke her up in the morning, so I had already said goodbye to her the night before. I knew I would not be seeing her for at least a year. When I traveled for work, I would be gone for one to two weeks at a time, but I had never been separated from my family for more than that. I was sad, I had many different emotions running inside my head, but I was determined to stay strong for the betterment of my daughter. I knew that by parting ways now, Jharana would have many new opportunities, would learn many new life skills, and, most of all, would learn to be a strong, independent, and responsible young lady, as Kamala and I had always hoped. This was our dream for both of our daughters.

As soon as Peter arrived, I grabbed my luggage and walked out the door. We left the house quietly, but a part of me had still not left Falmouth. The whole trip to the airport was not easy. I stayed quiet for some time and tried to occupy my mind with all the opportunities Jharana would have these coming years. That got me excited for her. Jharana was in my mind the entire trip back to the airport. That short trip felt hours long. How would she feel when she woke up in the morning? While riding with Peter, I was trying to analyze Jharana's new environment, her new school, her host family, the new culture, new language, and many other challenges she could be facing that year at the school.

अनुकुल बेदनीयम् सुखम् प्रतिकुल बेदनीयम् दुखम्

The above Sanskrit quote seems to perfectly fit this situation: "The same situation can make a person happy or sad." Looking at the positivity of the situation at that time it was a moment of great happiness for me as our dream of providing her good education and enabling her to lead her life independently was coming to fruition. On the other hand, I was sad to leave her in a foreign country by herself. It was difficult for me to leave my vulnerable teenage daughter in a foreign country halfway around the world, but I knew she would be in good hands. I left Falmouth with a heavy heart, but deep inside I knew it was the best decision for my daughter.

Falmouth Academy turned out to be a very good school. The teachers were caring and friendly. They did not hesitate to give Jharana some extra time when she was having problems with her schoolwork. One teacher even offered to take Jharana to the mall once when she saw she was homesick. Mary Sellers was a very caring host mother. Shauna, Jharana's host sister, was a few years younger than Jharana, which was also helpful, as that reminded of her home and her younger sister.

Jharana graduated from Falmouth Academy in 1994. The headmaster, Bruce Buxton, came to know that Jharana had a younger sister ready to go to high school. He called me one day and asked me if I was interested in sending Archana to his school as well. I was overjoyed! The school offered to search for a host family for Archana. We did not have to pay for anything except the plane fare, her pocket expenses, and money for books and school supplies. Archana then followed in her sister's footsteps.

Archana was hosted by the Schwarzman family during her two years at Falmouth Academy. The Schwarzmans, Beth and Gary, had two daughters who had already graduated from Falmouth Academy and were away at college, yet they continued to be dedicated members of the school community at that time. Archana still recalls the time when Beth patiently stayed up late at night with her, reading and explaining passages from Barbara Tuchman's American history book line by line. We couldn't have asked for better guardians for Archana during her time in Falmouth and beyond.

The Innocence

Early in the 1990s, I made a trip to visit several volunteers in the Eastern Development Region. I had allotted about twenty days to visit eight volunteers in the Sunsari, Tehrathum, Taplejung, and Sankhuwasabha districts. From Kathmandu the driver and I drove all the way to Dharan in one day. It was a long drive, but we preferred not to spend an extra night on the road. In Dharan, I found out that Pushpa, an American Peace Corps volunteer of Indian origin, was more involved in health-related activities than with her assigned teacher training job. She was spending her time taking physically disabled children to the Hospital and Rehabilitation Center for Disabled Children (HRDC) in Banepa for surgery and rehabilitation afterward. HRDC provided free medical and surgical services, and she paid their other expenses on her own. Pushpa had tapped into different sources of funding, then added her own money to help the disabled children of the poorest families of Dharan. While I was concerned that Pushpa was spending less time on her training duties than was expected by the Ministry of Education, I was impressed by her genuine dedication to the disabled children.

I was then involved with HRDC as voluntary executive member of the board of directors. HRDC treats physically disabled children under the age of fourteen. The staff conducts field visits to identify disabled children, bringing them to Banepa hospital if they cannot be treated locally. They are evaluated and have surgery if needed. After surgery they start rehabilitation at the hospital before returning to their own community, where the staff visits to check on their progress and reinforce what they have learned. All of this is free if the family cannot afford the cost.

After spending time with Pushpa, I drove up to Tehrathum. I spent a day with Jim in Myanglung, then headed toward Taplejung. I spent a day in Hangpang with John and another day in Sinam with Jenny. The visits went well. Both of them were doing well and were happy with their jobs and living situations even though they were living on *dal, bhat,* and *saag* as their staple meal.

After my trip to Taplejung, I came back to Chainpur in Sankhu-wasabha district to visit three more volunteers. Ted was assigned to the high school in Chainpur. The other two volunteers were assigned to high schools in Aankhibhui and Tamaphok. This was the end of my trip, and my backpack was not so heavy, as I had unloaded the mail and gift packages for the volunteers I had visited. Even then I did not feel like carrying my backpack, so I asked the headmaster to send the school office helper with me all the way to the roadhead. I told the headmaster that I would give the office helper some money on top of food expenses. The school had to buy some supplies, so the office helper would return with a load as well. It worked out very well. The office helper was happy with the extra money, he had never been to the tarai, and it was a chance for him to see a big bazaar.

We headed toward the roadhead. From Chainpur we had to go to Rambeni to catch the jeep that was waiting for me. On our way to the roadhead, the office helper told me that he had never been out of his district. He had not seen an automobile in his life. He was very excited when I told him that he would be able to ride with us to Dharan. On our walk down the long hill, the office helper stood motionless watching the road for a few minutes and asked me, "Sir, how did those two trucks decide who is going which way without meeting and talking about it?" At first, I did not understand his question. Then he pointed toward two trucks going in opposite directions. I was astounded at his innocence. Even in our fast-moving world, this villager still didn't know how trucks could pass each other without colliding. I explained that there are certain rules that must be observed by drivers to avoid accidents.

Who is happier? The innocent people who lack simple knowledge, or the people running after the latest tech gadget?

The Attitude

Matt was one of the most intelligent and most experienced science teachers among the volunteers. He was assigned to a high school in the eastern hills of Nepal, where he was conducting several training programs for Nepali science teachers in the construction and use of low-cost/no-cost science equipment. He had shared his new ideas about teaching science in Nepali schools with me, and he was keen to share his ideas with the interested officials at the Ministry of Education (MOE).

When Matt was in Kathmandu, he asked me if I could set up an appointment for him with the secretary of education to share some of his ideas about teaching science and also to discuss how these ideas could be shared with science teachers in other districts. I had set up an appointment with the secretary of education for 11:30 that morning. Matt arrived at my office at 10:45 a.m. wearing old jeans that probably had not been washed for several months and had a big hole near his left knee. When I reminded him about our appointment, he said he was ready and that was why he had come to my office. I pointed at his clothes and asked him how he could visit the secretary at his office with that kind of outfit.

He took it very lightly and said, "Ambika, I am a volunteer. I don't have money to wear fancy clothes. Of course, I don't wear these jeans to my classroom."

I was surprised that he thought the clothes he was wearing were not appropriate for his classroom but were all right for the meeting with the secretary of education. I asked him a question. "Matt, would this outfit be appropriate for a meeting with the secretary of education in the US? If not, what would you wear for that kind of meeting in America?"

He said he would certainly have a suit and tie for a meeting with the secretary of education in America. Then I requested that he go home and change his clothes. I would postpone the meeting until the afternoon. I told him that I couldn't take him to the Ministry of Education that way. He was not happy. He made many excuses. He told me that he had not brought any other clothes from his post. The jeans that he was wearing were the only pair of pants that he had here in Kathmandu. I arranged to advance him some money from his monthly allowance, had him buy a pair of pants, and rescheduled the appointment for the following week.

Volunteers live with a basic living allowance, which is not much different from their Nepali counterpart coworker's salary. The Peace Corps conducts a living allowance survey every few years and adjusts the amount accordingly. If the survey shows a need to increase the living allowance by a large amount, then Peace Corps / Nepal has to get approval from Peace Corps / Washington. In this way, the volunteers' living standard is kept on par with that of their local coworkers.

Volunteers often think that since they are volunteers, they should be able to live any way they want. However, even though they are volunteers, they have to abide by the rules, regulations, and cultural norms of the country. Not abiding by cultural norms could be viewed as either negligence or irresponsibility on the part of the volunteers. Being a volunteer is a two-way street. The volunteers sacrifice their time and the salary that they could have earned at home and are required to have a respectful attitude toward their service to their host country. At the same time, they benefit from their exposure to developing countries. Many volunteers have stated that they received much more than they gave to the community that they served. They were exposed to a third-world country's problems and learned to see the world from the perspective of someone from a different culture. Their Peace Corps experience may even qualify them for a future job in government service, the corporate world, or other international nongovernmental organizations (INGOs).

Early Terminations (ET)

The majority of volunteers join the Peace Corps to serve, and most of them are very serious about their commitment. At the time of the Vietnam War, though, some joined to dodge the draft. In the sixties and early seventies, due to the popularity of Eastern spirituality in the West, some joined hoping for spiritual happiness and peace of mind. But if their expectations weren't met, some did terminate their service. Few volunteers left before their two years had ended. Volunteers could leave for any reason. The attrition rate in Nepal was between 7 and 10 percent. Among the young volunteers, a relationship with a boyfriend or girlfriend was usually the reason people left early.

Others could not adjust to the culture. I know of one volunteer who decided to go back immediately after landing at Tribhuwan International Airport. In this case, I really don't know why he took the trouble to come all the way to Nepal only to turn back.

While doing post surveys, we tried to get as much information as possible about the post. Available housing facilities, food supply, medical facilities, and recommendations of previous volunteers and teaching staff were all included in the survey form that was provided to the volunteers. Despite all this information, sometimes volunteers found the information incomplete and terminated their service because something was lacking. The Peace Corps tried to accommodate volunteers by transferring them to a new post. I remember two specific cases of volunteers who could not give me a valid reason for terminating their services.

On Christmas Eve, three volunteers walked into my office and said they had a good Christmas present for me. They had been sworn in just a few days before and had gone to their posts immediately after the swearing-in ceremony. All three of them spent a night at the post and returned to Kathmandu. I did not even know they were back in town. However, it looked as if they had already made up their minds to leave before they had even been to their posts. I wondered how they could make such a critical decision without even seeing where they were going to serve. I thought that if they had stayed for a few more weeks, they could have made a more informed decision and benefited from learning at least a little about Nepal. But it was up to them to make their decision.

The second case was Jack, a volunteer who came to me after a few weeks at his post in Surkhet, saying that Coca-Cola was not available in the market as was written in the post survey form, and for this reason he wished to leave. I thought this was a joke at first. On second thought, I knew it was just an excuse. Later on, I found out that he had been trying to call his girlfriend from Surkhet, and in those days, phone service was not easily available. Sometimes we even had to telegraph from Kathmandu to the district centers using international Morse code. Jack's friends told me that he was very serious about his girlfriend and that he had planned to call her at least once a week, which was impossible in those days from Surkhet.

Volunteers or trainees who decided to quit had a few days to prepare for their departure, collect their belongings from their posts, and have a medical check. They received a plane ticket to the nearest airport to their home. In very rare cases, the country director could make a decision to give them money instead of a plane ticket so that the volunteer could travel a little bit on their way back home. Among the volunteers, early termination or administrative separation was known as the "Pan Am award back home." Alas, Pan Am flights are no more. Pan American World Airways was the unofficial flag carrier of the United States until it collapsed in December 1991.

Travel

Every year the Peace Corps conducted regional conferences for program officers working in all countries where the Peace Corps had programs. There were conferences covering specific programs like education, agriculture, health, and rural development, as well as Peace Corps general administration and other topics. Sometimes the Peace Corps included staff from different regions in the same conference. Every year at least a few program officers from each country had a chance to travel to another Peace Corps country and meet colleagues from other countries as well as staff from Peace Corps / Washington. All these conferences provided a venue for exchanging ideas and learning from one another.

One year, the Peace Corps held a worldwide conference in Lome, Togo, a small Francophone country in Western Africa that was a French colony until 1960. Three of us from Nepal participated in that conference.

On our way to Togo, we had a layover in Paris for one night. Thai Airlines provided us with a hotel and transportation to and from the airport, but we were on our own for food. That evening we took a short walk to enjoy the beautiful city. The women seemed dressed as if they were going to a party even though they were just walking on the street. It was midsummer, a perfect time to expose their beautiful bodies. We young men were pleased that the French "leggy beauties" were out there for exhibition.

Language was a problem, as none of us knew any French, and the French people we met did not want to speak English. We found only a few people who were willing to have a short conversation in English with us. So we spent our time in Paris looking at pedestrians and visiting a few tourist sites.

The next morning we had a few hours of free time before heading to the airport, so we decided to go window shopping. After a few hours of walking, we looked for a small restaurant to have breakfast. My friend had a hangover from the previous night's drinking. We walked into a restaurant and asked for a menu. We soon realized that nobody in the restaurant spoke any English. We couldn't figure out any of the items on the menu. The only two words we understood were "fish" and "beer." I wanted to go to another restaurant, but my friend kept insisting that he wanted to try whatever was available there. He might have thought a little beer would help his hangover. We ordered fish and beer. The fish was as solid as a rock and very salty—it turned out that dried, salted fish is a delicacy there. We realized how big a problem it was that we couldn't speak French. We found another restaurant where a waiter spoke some broken English. We ate our breakfast there. After breakfast we went back to the hotel, where a limousine was waiting for us to go to the airport.

I had heard about hundreds of historical and religious sites that attract tourists in Paris, but I had to be happy with whatever I was able to see. You can't always get what you want, but if you try sometimes, you might find you get what you need. (Rolling Stones)

On our way to Togo, due to a technical problem with our flight, we had a twenty-four-hour layover in Abidjan, Ivory Coast. Abidjan is the economic capital of the Ivory Coast and a cultural hub of West Africa. The Ivory Coast was a French colony until independence in 1960. In our free time in Abidjan, we wanted to do some sightseeing. We asked some local people about places we should see. Strangely enough, they suggested one of the places that we must see was Hotel Cote d'Ivoire, the hotel where we were staying. It was so big that it had its own ice-skating rink. Walking from one restaurant to another took us fifteen minutes when we decided to go for dessert after dinner that night. No wonder that hotel was a tourist attraction!

The central business district of Abidjan is rich with attractively designed skyscrapers. This city is not only a transit point for travelers traveling to and from sub-Saharan Africa, it also has interesting sites that are worth taking some extra time to visit. We did not get a chance to visit any of these sites as we did not have much time in Abidjan. From Abidjan our next stop was Lome, where our conference had been planned. Lome is a small town. Our conference was held in Hotel de la Paix, the biggest hotel in town. It was an international conference with many Peace Corps / Washington staff and participants from Peace Corps offices all around the world. Ten days went by so quickly. We ate couscous and walked around the town in our free time.

We wanted to see some of the interesting geographical and historical sights of Togo in the vicinity of Lome but did not have enough time to do so. Lome is a beautiful city with friendly people and has a very different culture from what I had experienced in my life so far. I had never been to Africa, and this visit was my first and only to a country of predominantly black people. In our conference it was different, as we had people from all around the world. We could not spend enough time to truly understand their culture, but we enjoyed everything we saw.

One thing that I still remember is strolling through the bazaar, which reminded me of the *haat* bazaars in Terai towns in Nepal. The dried fish, green vegetables, fruits and grains, and other foods certainly reminded me of the Nepali haat bazaar. We also loved seeing the African wood carvings in the Lome bazaar. An interesting place to visit.

Thai Hospitality

Whenever I have to change planes between international flights, I go to the airline counter to make sure my luggage has been transferred. But on my flight back from Lome to Paris, the time between landing and takeoff was so short that I did not have enough time to inquire about my luggage. I only had time to run from one terminal to the other to catch my flight. I was the last passenger to board the plane. I was hopeful that they were able to transfer my luggage onto the plane going to Bangkok. Two of us Nepalese and one American attended the conference. I returned on a Thai flight to Kathmandu via Bangkok, and the other participants took another route.

I arrived in Bangkok in the late afternoon and found that my luggage had not arrived. As I had feared, they had not had enough time to upload it in Paris. The Thai staff assured me that they would call their office in Paris and make sure that the luggage would come on the next day's flight. They provided me with two choices: either go to Kathmandu the next day and wait for the luggage in Kathmandu or wait in Bangkok for two days. They guaranteed me that the luggage would be there in Bangkok before my flight on the third day, and they would pay for my hotel and food for two days' stay in Bangkok. I decided to wait in Bangkok for two days even though it was Dashain time. I didn't want to lose my baggage. The Thai International staff was very courteous, and they did whatever they could to make my stay in Bangkok comfortable and pleasant. I went to the hotel and rested for a while. I was quite upset and so tired I did not feel like eating dinner, so I went down to the bar and asked for a Singha (a local Thai beer). I sat down at a table and started reading a book while I drank the beer.

A Thai gentleman approached me and asked if he could join me. I had never met this gentleman, but before I said anything, he sat down in the chair opposite to me and also ordered a beer. He likely figured out from my expression and behavior that I was not happy that day. He politely asked me what I was doing in Bangkok. I explained about my trip and told him I had lost my baggage on my way from Paris. We sat for quite a long time talking about Thailand and Nepal and our jobs, our families, and other topics. He (Anuman) told me that he worked as a curator for the Chulalongkorn University museum.

I think we had quite a few beers before we parted. Before leaving the bar, he extended an invitation for the next day to have breakfast at his house and a tour of Bangkok with his family. I was hesitant, as it was our first meeting, but because of his insistence, I had no choice but to accept his invitation. Early the next morning, he arrived at my hotel to take me to his house. He had a nice house in the outskirts of Bangkok. He had a seven- or eight-year-old son and a beautiful wife. Apsara (his wife) was very polite and had prepared a tasty Thai breakfast of stir-fried chicken, boiled pork blood, rice pudding, rambutan, and some other fruits. He gave me a tour of downtown Bangkok, several *wats* (Buddhist temples), parks, and many other interesting places that day.

Around midday we stopped at gas a station to refill the car. As he was paying all the expenses, I thought I could at least pay for the gas, but he would not let me pay, saying that it was against Thai hospitality.

He also played the role of tour guide for me. Among the thousands of *wats* of Thailand, we visited Wat Phra Kaew, Wat Benchamabophit Dusitvanaram, and Wat Pho, which is also known as Wat Phra Chetuphon. Wat Pho is the Wat of the Reclining or Sleeping Buddha, which houses one thousand Buddha images from the ruins of the former capitals of Thailand, Ayuthaya, and Sukhothai. I was amazed by the way Thai people have preserved their wats and the way they show respect to their religion. I noticed that the *bhante* (Buddhist monks) in Thailand receive utmost respect from the Thai people. While traveling on a bus or any form of public transportation, people stand up and bow and vacate a seat for the *bhante*.

The Thai king is also very well respected in Thailand even though the country is governed by a constitutional monarchy and the king is just a figurehead. Kings in the current Chakri dynasty of Thailand are referred to as Rama, with a number following their name. Rama is taken from the Hindu epic Ramayana and is accepted as an incarnation of god Vishnu. The ruling monarch at that time was Bhumibol Adulyade, or King Rama the Ninth.

I suggested that we go for dinner at a good restaurant because I wanted to show my gratitude to them for being my tour guide from the early morning until late afternoon. We agreed that we would go to a floating restaurant for dinner. On our way back from one of the Wats, we had an accident. My host was driving about forty kilometers an hour, and we were talking and enjoying our time. While taking a left turn, a car coming from the other direction swerved in our direction and hit the rear end of our car. It was just a fender bender, but I was worried, as it could have been a big problem in Nepal. Both of the drivers stopped, got out, and inspected their cars. Then I saw them bowing to each other. They talked for a few minutes and swapped business cards and left. I could not believe how polite they were being, so I asked him for details. He told me that they had agreed to meet the next day during office hours and settle the issue. What trust they had of people whom they had never met before!

We had a long day, and the tour was fascinating. I had had a university museum curator as my private guide. He was so knowledgeable about the history of wats that he did not have any problem explaining when and how the wats were built, the history of the wats, and how they preserve them. I was quite impressed. Apsara was a teacher by profession and was also very polite and courteous with me that whole day.

Anuman dropped me at the hotel. After I rested awhile, they came to pick me up, and we drove to the beach. The restaurant was a big, beautiful ferry boat that had been turned into a restaurant. As usual I ordered seafood, as we do not get seafood in Nepal. We had some wine and appetizers to start. While we were eating, I noticed him going to the restroom. When we were about to finish our meal, I went to the counter on the pretext of going to the restroom and inquired about our bill. He had beaten me here too. He had already paid the bill while going to the restroom. Until today, I have not been able to figure out if his kindness was due to Thai culture or just him. His hospitality, his courteous behavior, the politeness of the family, and their welcoming attitude to a stranger made me think very highly of Thai people and their hospitality.

I left Thailand not only with my baggage but also with a strong impression of this beautiful country, full of polite, courteous, well-behaved, respectful, and down-to-earth people with unprecedented hospitality, a true reflection of the Buddhist religion. I offer my salutation to this wonderful culture.

Come with the Marines

The assistant training officer came to my office one early Thursday morning begging me to help him by going to Trishuli so I could ask the secondary master trainer (SMT) to let us use his facility for our training. He said he had been to Trishuli twice before and had tried to convince the SMT with no success.

Having been in the education program for a long time, I had a good relationship with most of the ministry and district education officials. As such, the assistant training officer thought I might be able to persuade the SMT to allow us to train in his facility. I had no idea about the compensation paid for the use of training facilities. I talked to the assistant training officer about all the details because I did not want to offer the SMT anything we could not provide. At the same time, I also went to talk to the administrative officer to find out if he had any more guidelines for such an agreement. With this information I felt prepared to try to make the facility available for our training.

On Friday morning I told my secretary that I was going to Trishuli to see if I could get the Secondary Education Development Unit's (SEDU) facility for our training. It was about a three-and-a-half-hour drive each way. I left the office around 8:30 a.m. The road was bumpy and winding for most of the trip.

The SMT was happy to see me. We had tea and started talking about using his facility. At first he was hesitant to let us use it for two and a half months, but after some time, he agreed. I also had to find a technical trainer for the training program. Since he was the most suitable person for the job, I offered it to him, but he was a little reluctant, as this would be the first time he had trained foreigners to be mathematics and science teachers. After a while, he assured me that he would accept the job if he got approval from his supervisor. He had to get a leave of absence approved before he signed the contract to work for the

Peace Corps. I was happy with the outcome.

In those days, the Science Education Development Project had wisely selected all the best mathematics and science teachers as their trainers, and he was one of the best among them. I was happy that I had been able to finalize the deal, even though it took two hours. My long and tiring trip had been successful.

I arrived in Kathmandu just before the mail room closed, so I was able to check my mail before the close of business on Friday. I also told the training officer that a deal had been made with the Trishuli SMT for us to use the facility for our training and that the SMT was willing to work as a technical trainer.

"Why the hell did you go to Trishuli?"

I was surprised and shocked to hear these words from my boss. I was chatting with my colleagues before I went home that evening when the director came out to the parking lot and asked me this question. There were also some drivers and other junior staff around us at that time. Everybody looked at me as if I had committed a heinous crime. I asked him if we could talk, but he was not in a mood to talk. He just told me that we could talk on Monday morning. He looked very upset, but I did not know why. He spoiled my whole weekend, as I kept trying to figure out what was going on.

I soon learned that he was going to Bangkok that evening with a sick volunteer. It is usually the medical officer's responsibility to accompany a volunteer for medical evacuation to Bangkok or Washington, DC. In this case, the medical officer could not accompany the volunteer, and most of the program officers were in the field, so the country director had to accompany the volunteer to Bangkok. He was on his way home to grab his luggage.

I went home, but I was pondering his question the whole weekend. What did he really mean? Why did he ask me that question? Nothing came to mind. Maybe he was upset because I was not available to talk about accompanying the sick volunteer. I was anxiously waiting for Monday to come, as the director was coming back from Bangkok on Sunday evening, and I really wanted to find out what had inspired him to ask me that question. I was unsure how to approach him.

First thing on Monday morning, I called the director and asked him if I could see him. "Come with the marines" was his answer. I could not figure out what he was trying to say. Maybe he meant come prepared for our discussion.

I jokingly asked, "Why marines? I might come with the Gurkhas."

We had a very good conversation. It did not take long to figure out that the problem had been that our training officer had not wanted to show that his own office could not make the deal. A cultural problem. The training officer was American, and the assistant training officer was Nepali. When the Nepali assistant training officer sought assistance, the American training officer probably thought it demonstrated his inability to handle the situation. I found out that the American training officer had complained to the country director about my trip to Trishuli, even though I had gone there at his assistant's request. The training officer had told the director that I had crossed boundaries and was stepping in his area. It was cleared up after the director called the assistant training officer and the administrative officer to explain why and how I had gone to Trishuli. Both of them explained that I had a long and clear discussion with them before my trip. The assistant training officer also explained that I had gone to Trishuli at his request, as he was having a problem working out the deal with the SMT in Trishuli.

Consolation

Cathy explained to me in a very sad mood that ever since she had arrived here in Jaljale a month ago, five or six children would follow her every day on her way to school chanting *"Habsi, habsi, kali, kali."* She was very frustrated and tried different methods to get the children to stop this irritating chanting and taunting. These children were four or five years old, and none of them were enrolled in school. She did not understand the meaning of the words *habsi* and *kali*. She asked the teachers at the school, but no one explained the real meaning of the words. Probably they did not want to upset her.

The Peace Corps is an equal opportunity employer and discrimination based on race, sexual orientation, color, age, and ethnicity is not tolerated, and affirmative action is taken to recruit qualified women, minorities, and disabled individuals. Most recruitment activities were planned on college campuses, and volunteers were usually fresh college graduates in their early twenties. Cathy was a black woman who had never been out of the US.

This was my first visit with Cathy after she got to her village. I had been to her village before, but not since she had arrived. Jaljale was a village in Tehrathum with a high school and a small store and a tea shop. Cathy was doing her teaching job well, but she was having problems with other villagers as well as the children. People in the villages thought that all black people were from Africa and that an American couldn't be black, so for them she must be an African. *Kali* means black female. *Habsi* is a derogatory word for black person in Nepali. Probably the children learned these taunting words from their parents. I talked to the headmaster and some of the village elders that afternoon. I asked them how they would feel if the group of children follow them saying *"Bahun katha"* for the Brahmin teachers and *"Newar Kode"* for the Newar teachers. These are two derogatory phrases used in Nepali hill towns for different ethnic groups of the country. Furthermore, I asked them how they would feel if that happened in a situation where they were new and lonely. How would they react? I tried to give them a picture of Cathy's situation in their village. I told them that Cathy was there at their request. Cathy had given up her family, friends, her education, and many more lucrative chances in America in order to help Nepali students for two years. She did not sacrifice her comfortable life in America to be teased by children here in Nepal. I asked them how they would feel if they were in Cathy's situation. I told them that it is their responsibility to provide her support, not harass her. They understood Cathy's problem. They promised me that they would take care of it, explaining to their children that Cathy was an American teacher who had come to Nepal at the invitation of the Nepal government and that they should respect her as a foreign teacher coming to help the community school.

I had a productive time with Cathy in Jaljale. She was happy with her situation and was doing a good job as a first-year math and science teacher. The headmaster and teachers were happy with her enthusiasm and the new activities she had introduced to her science classes, which some of the other teachers had adopted as well. It was only this situation of being taunted by the children that was problematic.

That evening Cathy and I went for dinner in a tea shop, which prepared food for travelers in the area. While we were eating our dal bhat, Tuki *didi*, the owner of the tea shop, stared at me as if something was puzzling her. Then she went inside to another room and came out with a picture in her hand. She handed me the picture and asked me if that was me. It was the wedding picture of Kamala and me at Budhnilkantha Temple, where our wedding had taken place. Tuki didi later explained that she was from Dhankuta and that her house was close to Kamala's, so she knew Kamala from childhood. Kamala's brother had given her the photo when she was in Dhankuta last time. What a coincidence! My wedding picture in the hand of a woman I had never seen in my life. I spent two days at Cathy's village and came back to Kathmandu. After that trip Cathy was happy and wrote me that she had not been taunted since then.

The photo Tuki didi showed us

Months later in Kathmandu, as we were preparing for our supervisors' conference, we received a cable from the US embassy saying "Cathy's grandmother passed away peacefully on Saturday, July 17. Cathy was very close to her grandmother and may need some assistance to cope with this unexpected demise of her grandmother. Please pass this message to her and provide needed assistance."

All the education volunteers and their Nepali supervisors (high school headmasters and counterpart Nepali teachers) were in Kathmandu to participate in the conference. The conference was scheduled to clarify any cross-cultural misunderstandings between volunteers and the Nepali teachers, strengthen working relationships, provide tips on

teaching in Nepali schools, and other items that volunteers felt needed to be addressed. This was the first time Cathy's group had been to
Kathmandu after completing training in December. They had not seen
many of the other volunteers for the past six months.

I left a message in Cathy's mailbox asking her to come to see me
early the next day. As her Peace Corps supervisor, I was responsible for
informing her about her grandmother. After talking with her about her
village, her work, and other issues in her village, I told her I had sad
news for her and handed her the cable. I waited for her reaction. Slowly her face changed. She didn't say a single word for a while, but tears
started rolling down her cheeks. She kept quiet for a few minutes. She
read the cable again and she asked, sobbing, why her family did not
call her and why the message came through official channels instead.

I was in an awkward situation. I started consoling her, but then I
remembered a cross-cultural session we had in staff training. "If someone is having a problem like a death in the family or the serious injury
of a family member because of involvement in an accident, the person
may need some time to gather himself or herself and may want to cry.
Let him or her cry. Crying helps them to deal with the situation."

Then I told Cathy, "Cathy, you may need some time on your own
to deal with the situation. I am going to leave you here, and I will come
back in half an hour, and we can talk about it. Then we will discuss
how the Peace Corps can help you."

When I came back, she had stopped crying, but her face still looked
very sad. Now she looked like she was ready for some conversation.

Communication in Nepal in those days was not that developed.
Our communication with Peace Corps / Washington took place
through the State Department cable system. Volunteers had the priv-
ilege of getting messages through this channel in case of emergencies
and in urgent financial circumstances. It would have taken at least two
weeks for Cathy to get this message through the regular mail.

There is a cultural difference in the way Americans and Nepalis react in this kind of situation. If a Nepali has a death or serious illness in his/her family, we stay with the person and try to console him/her, telling them that it is the way of life. People come and go. We have to live with it. By contrast, I was trained not to spend much time with the volunteer at the beginning but to give her some time to work through it, to let her assess the situation and the incident. We should share the message, briefly discuss the situation with the volunteer, and, depending upon how the volunteer takes the issue, we may need to leave that person alone for a while.

This is probably an outcome of the way children are raised in the Western world. From a very young age, they are taught to be independent, whereas in our Eastern culture, we depend much more on our family and friends. In Nepal, friends, relatives, and even neighbors surround the person at the time of illness or death. If somebody is sick in the US, it is considered impolite for people other than close family and friends to ask about the illness, whereas in our society, we try to find out as much as we can and do not hesitate to prescribe our own solution or medicines for the disease even though we may not have any medical background.

Cathy then asked about emergency leave. According to Peace Corps regulations, if a death occurs in a volunteer's immediate family, the Peace Corps grants a leave of absence for the volunteer and pays for the volunteer's round trip home. But in Cathy's case, her grandmother was not listed as an immediate family member, so the Office of Special Services (OSS) did not approve her emergency leave.

OSS had a twenty-four-hour duty officer and twenty-four-hour emergency telephone line. If there was any problem at home, the relatives could call OSS for help and relay their message to the volunteer. OSS would handle the situation as professionally as possible. In case of a death in the immediate family, OSS would let us know immediately and at the same time inform us whether the volunteer qualified for emergency leave.

In Cathy's case, OSS had clearly indicated that emergency leave would not be paid for by Peace Corps, but that she could go for two weeks at her own expense. Cathy reluctantly decided to pay for her own trip.

Confrontation with the Maoists

It was November, and preservice training for the Peace Corps volunteers was in full swing. It looked like we had a good group of trainees and staff. The trainees were in language classes every morning for four hours. In the afternoon they had technical training, which involved lesson planning, practice teaching, and material development. Late afternoon was set aside for cross-cultural sessions. In these sessions, the cross-cultural coordinator discussed issues such as the concept of *jutho* and clarifying that same-sex friends who were holding hands were not necessarily gay in Nepali context. Women's "untouchability" during their periods and other issues were covered. They had a good introduction to Nepali culture in these sessions.

We had a total of thirty trainees in that group. I had already selected twenty-five posts for them, and I had to find out about ten more to have a few extras, so that they could choose a second one if they didn't like the first one. I had already made a trip to the western part of the country to develop sites for these volunteers. I had been to the training site for the last three days to observe and see how the training was going on. Now that I was assured that training was going well, I was ready to move on to the eastern hills to choose sites from among the requests we had received from the schools as well as from the Ministry of Education.

I was planning to go to Ilam, Panchthar, and Taplejung during that trip and expected to post two or three volunteers in each of those districts. I was planning to start checking the schools from Ilam and go all the way to Taplejung and back. Some of the schools were at the roadhead, and some were several hours' walk from the road.

I started from Dharan early in the morning, hoping to go all the way to Ilam Bazaar after completing the post survey in Phikal. Phikal was right on the road, and the school was just a few minutes' walk downhill from the roadhead. I had a good breakfast in Dharan, so I was not worried about lunch. The roadhead town had about thirty stores. The shops had a good selection of groceries and household items. The driver would have preferred to have his *tomba* (millet beer) here if he had finished driving for the day, but I knew he would not touch alcohol until we ended our journey for the day, and we had several hours' drive ahead of us. Anywhere you spend the night in these eastern hill districts, you never want to give up your share of *tomba*, as this part of the country is also known as Tombaland among the volunteers. I told the driver to go ahead and eat *dal bhat* at the roadhead teashop, as I was going to be gone for at least three hours collecting information for the post report.

Phikal is close to Darjeeling in India, which had been developed by the British into a beautiful hill station. Being close to Darjeeling and maybe from their association with the British in Darjeeling, the people of Phikal had learned to appreciate the beauty of flowers. Every house had flowers planted in the front. If there wasn't enough land, flowers were planted in flower pots. The town looked clean and beautiful.

The lush green tea gardens around the school and on both sides of the road looked like a green carpet covering the hills. The laborers were all women, plucking tea leaves and throwing them into *dokos* (baskets) on their backs, held by a *namlo* (a head strap sustaining a doko on their back). They were singing, laughing, joking, and making fun of one another other while working. It was not raining, but I could feel a refreshing mist in the air.

The walk from the roadhead to the school was pleasant. The trail led between the tea plantations in a serpentine fashion. There was a spectacular view of Kanchenjunga, the third-highest mountain in the world, 8,586 meters (28,169 feet) above sea level, visible through the clouds. The pristine white snow on Kanchenjunga looked close enough to touch. Though this was not the famous sunrise view of Kanchenjunga from Tiger Hill in Darjeeling, the scenic tea gardens in the foreground gave this view its own beauty.

I walked slowly, taking time to enjoy the beautiful scenery. When I reached the school, the school office helper prevented me from entering the headmaster's office and asked me to wait outside. I was surprised. This had never happened to me before. I asked the office helper what was going on. He told me in a hushed voice that there were some people inside the headmaster's office. That made me more curious.

I asked the office helper who those people were, but he did not want to talk. They were talking loudly, but I could not make out the words. Once in a while I heard a teenage female voice, strong, and persuasive. A young female shouting at the headmaster at his office was unusual in Nepal. I was even more curious.

Eventually the office helper asked me to go to the teachers' office. They looked uncomfortable. Usually the teachers' room is full of lively chatter between class periods. I went to sit with a teacher I knew from a previous visit. In a quiet voice he told me that there were some Maoist students in the headmaster's office. He told me that he did not know what they were talking about but that they had been there for over an hour.

I was puzzled. I had high hopes of posting a volunteer in this school. Now it seemed that Maoist students were accusing the headmaster of something. Would it be safe to post a volunteer at a site where Maoists could shout at the headmaster without fear of consequences? The government had outlawed Maoist activities, and the Maoist Communist party of Nepal had been banned. There had also been a red corner notice by Interpol (International Criminal Police Organization) against the Maoist leaders. This was a letter to inform member countries of crimes committed by individuals and groups, requesting them to arrest these people if they saw them. The Nepali police had a standing order to arrest any Maoists they came across.

The volunteers' safety was our primary concern. We would never post a volunteer to any village where we could not guarantee their safety. Now I was in a dilemma. Should I wait and find out what was going on? Or just say goodbye and leave, and find another village where I would not have to worry about safety and security issues for volunteers?

I was not able to decide what my next step should be. Then I saw two boys and one girl coming out of the headmaster's office. Luckily, I thought quickly enough to approach them and ask them if I could talk to them for a few minutes. They looked at me and looked at each other, wondering who I was. After a while, the oldest of the three, who looked to be in his twenties, asked me to follow him to the school volleyball court. The grounds were empty, as class was in session. The other two followed us.

We sat down on the ground. They glanced at each other, hesitant to speak. Then I told them who I was and asked them who they were and why they were there. Finally, the girl opened her mouth and explained that they were student union (Maoists wing) members. They said that there had been a rumor that school funds had been embezzled. They had been talking to the headmaster about that, and the headmaster had agreed to open the account book to the public. At the village committee meeting the coming week, people would be able to look at the account book and ask questions.

I was glad to know what they were doing even though they were not officially authorized to check the school accounts. The auditor from the district education office should have done this kind of work, not the student union members.

Then I explained to them the purpose of my trip. I told them that I would not be able to post a volunteer in their school if the Maoist activities were so visible that the volunteer's safety and security was at stake. They asked me to give them about ten minutes to discuss it among themselves.

After more than a half hour, they came back and told me that all three of them were alumni of that school and that they would never think of doing anything that would tarnish the school's name. They assured me that they would guarantee the safety and security of the volunteer on one condition. They assured me that there would be no problem on their level but that if their head office in Kathmandu did not approve of that volunteer, we would get about five days' notice to remove volunteer from the village. They also told me that volunteers had taught them when they were students at that school and that they appreciated their teaching methods. They also told me that they had no negative feelings about the volunteers. Rather, they appreciated the hard work that the volunteers had been doing in Nepali schools.

I was not in a situation to make a decision right then and there. I told them that I had to consult with my office. I was relatively sure that there would not be a problem in that village, but I did not want to take a chance. I then went to talk with the headmaster. I saw him in his normal self. He explained everything that had happened. He assured me that there was no problem with the accounts, that he was ready to show the books to anybody at any time, and that the rumor would be cleared up at the next week's village committee meeting. He also assured me that there should be no problem with the volunteer's safety in the village. After I finished my survey form, he took me to meet some village leaders, and they unanimously assured me that there would be no problem and that they would guarantee the safety of the volunteer.

Even then, I was hesitant to post a volunteer where there were known Maoist students. What would happen if they didn't keep their word? What would happen if their head office did not give me enough time to pull out the volunteer? What would happen if there was some kind of confrontation between the Maoists and the police? The volunteer could be at the wrong place at the wrong time, even though the two parties would not be targeting the volunteers. There were lots of questions coming to my mind, and I did not have all the answers.

Should I present the issue at our country staff meeting? Should I explain the situation to the volunteers at our posting meeting, when they would be asked to choose from the available posts? How could we manage the risks and make sure that the volunteer would be safe for his/her two-year assignment and meet the need for a trained teacher at the village school?

The Maoist students had been positively impacted by the previous volunteers. They praised the volunteers' personal sacrifices to help Nepali students, undergoing conditions that were so unlike their life in America. I decided to wait to make any decision about choosing Phikal until I returned to Kathmandu and shared my concerns in our staff meeting.

Contemplation

With a long day's walk ahead of me, I started at around ten in the morning. It was a hot and sweltering summer day. I was on my way to a small village called Kaphalpani in Salyan district. The trail was narrow and twisted all around the hills, back and forth, up and down. The snow-capped mountains were visible whenever I approached the northern slope of the hills. Down below the trail lay a deep gorge marked with the course of a river. Tall trees and shrubs full of green foliage extended for miles on both sides of the path, which made the walk pleasant. Lush green forest and birdsong enhanced the charm of the trek. Even though it was the middle of the day, the trail led through the forest, and it was a little bit cooler and more pleasant than what I had expected.

My backpack full of mail and supplies for the Volunteers

I was carrying a backpack, which weighed about twenty-five pounds, containing my sleeping bag, clothes, a few cans of food for the volunteer, and her mail. We would usually take coffee, peanut butter, chocolate, bread, and tuna, which were treats for the volunteers, as nothing of this sort was available at their villages. It was like a Christmas package for them.

I had two more hours of walking before I got to the village. I was lost in my thoughts. The possible situation of the volunteer occupied my thoughts. I was thinking about her living situation, food arrangements, her mail, and so on. There were a lot of things that volunteers need to take care of in their villages. Water supply was a problem in most of the villages, and potable water was not easily available. They had to either treat their water with iodine or boil it for twenty minutes. And even for that water, they might have to walk an hour.

Some volunteers paid for the food, tuition, and books for poor students, and in exchange the students cooked for the volunteers and carried water for them. In some cases, these students might continue getting support from the volunteers until they completed their higher education. Many volunteers continued providing this kind of support years after they completed their service in Nepal and were back home in America. A good exchange.

All of a sudden, I heard a very loud thump, and a huge boulder landed in front of me. It had just rolled down the hill from above. I had heard no noise until it landed in front of me. Then I heard someone yelling from up above the hill, "Careful. A rock is coming down."

I stood there in shock, shaking with fear. I could not figure out what was going on, and I did not know what to do. The rock had almost hit me on my head. If I had been five steps ahead of where I was, I would have been killed right then and there. I stood there in fear for a few seconds and then ran backward on the path.

Then I stopped and looked ahead at the rock. Various thoughts

---

crossed my mind. I was still shaking with fear. After a few minutes, I tried to walk forward, but my feet were not moving properly. Somehow, I managed to walk around the rock, continuing until I got to a *chautari*, a resting place on the trail with a big *pipal* tree (Latin name Ficus Religiosa of the Moraceae family) and a *bar* tree (Banyan, Rosales, also Moraceae). Different parts of the pipal tree are said to be Brahma, Vishnu, and Maheshwor or Shiva (the gods of creation, protection, and destruction). In the Bhagavad Gita, Krishna says, "Of all the trees, I am the *pipal* tree." Hindus worship both the pipal and bar trees. These trees are also considered sacred in Buddhism. Before motor roads were built, chautari with pipal and bar trees were resting places for travelers.

I threw my backpack off and sat on a rock on the *chautari*. I was lost, scared, horrified, and shocked. I did not know what to do. I took out my water bottle and drank its contents in one gulp.

I don't remember how long I sat with my head resting in my hands. The minute I raised my head, I saw a man standing in front of me. He sat down next to me and asked me what had happened, as he saw me shaking, afraid, still in shock. I was sweating, and my clothes were all wet. I was trying to say something, but words would not come. He looked at my face and asked again what happened. I slowly collected myself and pointed my finger at the big rock. I explained what had happened. I told him that I just escaped from the mouth of death by a hair's width. I explained him where I was going and why.

He happened to be a local man going back home from his farm. He explained that they had a drinking water project going on and that they were digging ditches to lay pipes. They had received money from the district development committee, and UNICEF had donated the pipes and other supplies for the project. I was listening to him, but I did not really hear what else he said. I was still trembling and thinking about my life. I could have died right there, and it would have taken days just to get the news to my family and my office. I started questioning what I was doing and why I was walking alone on that remote path.

I slowly gathered myself, picked up my backpack, and resumed my journey. But the thought of the rock hitting me on my head did not go away. I was walking, but the thoughts kept coming. "OK, that is it. The minute I get back to Kathmandu, I am going to my office and tender my resignation. No, I cannot do this job if it means risking my life. I have a wife and daughters. What would happen to them if I die on a village trail? Who would take care of them?" I was lost in contemplation until I reached the volunteer's dera.

It took about two hours to get to the village. The man who had stopped at the *chautara* led me to the village and took me to the volunteer's dera. I was still having a hard time returning to normal. The volunteer asked me what was going on. I explained everything that had happened to me on the way to the village. I didn't tell her I had decided to resign, but I was determined to do so as soon as I got back to Kathmandu. I just could not imagine continuing this job even though I would have a very hard time finding another job that I would enjoy as much as this one. For me, the best aspect of my job was that with no financial burden on the Nepali government, we provided trained mathematics and science teachers that the villagers needed so badly. And I really did enjoy visiting the volunteers at their posts.

I finished my visit with the volunteer the second day. She was doing well and had no problems. The headmaster was happy with her teaching except that she was giving a hard time to the teachers who did not teach the full forty-five-minute periods. Some teachers would walk into the classroom, teach for part of the period, and then go to the office to socialize. The headmaster asked me to remind the volunteer that it was not the volunteer's job to look after the administration of the school.

The next day, I started my journey back to Kathmandu. It took me three days. I was still serious about quitting my job, but as the days passed, I forgot to tender my resignation. I did not tell Kamala about this incident. I knew that she would have worried whenever I traveled, and I was traveling six to seven months a year. I knew she would have forced me to quit my job rather than take such risks. My daughters would not have understood, as they were very young at that time.

Every coin has two faces. I decided to look at the brighter side and hang on to the job I was enjoying so much.

Culture Shock

I was on my way to visit Suzanne, a volunteer who was teaching mathematics and science in a village high school. She was in her midtwenties and had some Native American heritage. As with almost all her colleagues, this was her first trip out of the US. She knew that I was coming that day, but in Nepal, no matter how accurate you try to be, you may well reach your destination either a day early or a day late. It was almost dark when I reached the village. I was exhausted after walking in that long, hot summer day.

It was a small Gurung village. There was a cluster of houses on the side of a hill, all with thatched roofs. I had no problem finding her house. I saw a group of boys playing marbles. When I asked them where "American Miss" lived, one boy led me toward the house and pointed to it from a little distance. I was anxious to see how she was doing because she had been in the village for only five months and this was my first visit with her.

As I approached the house, I saw her sitting on the *pindhi* (a space just outside the front door of the house, a patio) with a cup of tea in her hand. She was so deeply lost in her thoughts that she did not notice my arrival. She had a paperback book and some pens and a few sheets of papers at her side. She might have been preparing her lesson plan for the next day and at the same time reading her book, but she didn't seem in the mood to do either.

"Hi, Suzanne. How are you doing?" I asked.

She was startled. She looked at me and screamed, "Am…bi…kaa!"

I took off my backpack and put it to the side. As I was taking off my sneakers, Suzanne said in very low voice, "Ambika, I have a serious problem." She was almost crying.

"What kind of problem? Are you homesick? Or are you having problems teaching? What is it?" As I had not taken off my shoes all day,

I wanted to wash my feet before I sat down for any serious talk. I asked her where the tap was.

She pointed to a tap next to the house, but at the same time she said, "Ambika, can we talk?"

Ambika on the way to visit volunteers

"Suzanne, that is why I am here. We have the whole night and the whole day tomorrow to talk. We certainly will have plenty of time to talk about everything. Let me wash my feet first, and then we can sit down and talk."

As soon as I said these few sentences, an old lady came out from the house and asked, "Who is this?"

Suzanne said, "This is Ambika, my *hakim* (boss) from Kathmandu."

The old lady asked, "Is he a Nepali or an American?"

"I'm a Nepali, aamaa (mother—kinship terms are used even for strangers)," I said.

The lady could not believe that I could also speak Nepali, as she had heard me speaking to Suzanne in English. It was already dark and the lady could not see me that well. She said, "You speak good Nepali."

I laughed and said, "I am a Nepali, and Nepali is my mother tongue."

I took out my soap and towel from my backpack and went to the tap to wash. I was surprised to see Suzanne in such a depressed mood. In training she had been outspoken, outgoing, and very friendly with all the language trainers and kitchen staff. She was, as we used to say, "perfect Peace Corps material." All the training staff thought that she would be a good volunteer. I had observed her practice teaching. She was very good in teaching and got along well with the students. She was culturally sensitive and had no problem adjusting during the twelve-week training period and the eight weeks of homestay. I was having a difficult time imagining what her problem could be.

As I came back from the tap, aamaa told us that dinner was ready. Rice, lentils, and *saag* (spinach). The food tasted good, maybe because I was hungry, as I had had nothing to eat after breakfast in Pokhara, other than a few cups of tea. Suzanne did not speak a single word while we ate our dal bhat. While we were eating, aamaa told me that Suzanne was doing well and liked Nepali food, but since last week she had not been eating well. She wanted me to find out if Suzanne did not like her cooking.

After dinner, Suzanne and I went out to the pindhi again, and I lit the candle I had brought. She could not believe how prepared I was for the village. I asked her several questions about her living situation, her food, school environment, and so on. Her answers were very short, "Yes" or "No." I was having a difficult time figuring out what was going on with her.

She told me she had gone to Pokhara for a weekend three months ago. She asked me whether I had received her absence-from-post form. She said she was in Pokhara for just two nights. She went there after school on Friday and came back Sunday evening. She had requested

Ramesh Sir to cover her math classes in fifth and sixth grades and Laxmi Miss to cover her seventh-grade science class on Sunday. She told me that Joe, Mike, Mary, and Dan were also there in Pokhara. She also told me that Mike came to visit her the next weekend. Mike was her nearest Peace Corps volunteer neighbor. I was glad to know that she was spending some time with other volunteers, which was essential for her sanity.

Around ten o'clock, Suzanne went to her room. I threw my sleeping bag on the floor and slept on the pindhi that night. In Nepali villages it is difficult to find a room, so I was used to sleeping on the volunteer's pindhi. It was a moonlit night. The stars were shining, and I was enjoying my time sleeping under the bright moonlight. I tried to read by candlelight for a while, but I gave up, as there was not enough light to read. I thought about Suzanne but could not figure out what was bothering her. I slept thinking I would have enough time to talk to her the next day.

The next day, after I observed her teaching and talked to the headmaster about her teaching and other activities, we came back to her dera. As Suzanne had not disclosed her problem yet, I decided to stay at her village for one more night, hoping that I would be able to help her solve her problem. After we got back home from school, aamaa gave us some popcorn and tea.

Again, we sat down at the pindhi, and I started the conversation. "OK, let us talk about your problem. You said you are having a serious problem, but you have not told me what it is yet."

Suzanne stared at my face but did not say anything. It seemed as though she didn't want to disclose her problem, but she had brought it up immediately after seeing me the first day in her village. I kept quiet for a while just to give her some time to put her thoughts together. Aamaa came out with some more popcorn and sat next to Suzanne. Aamaa said that she was very happy with Suzanne and accepted her as her own daughter. Aamaa's presence made it a little difficult to continue our conversation, but after a while, she went inside, saying it was time to prepare dinner.

I was thinking about how to start my conversation with Suzanne. All of a sudden, Suzanne broke into tears, saying, "I don't want ET (early termination). I don't want a Pan Am award."

I was confused. I did not know what she meant. I saw her face turn red and tears pouring down. I had no way out but deal with the issue. So I told her, "Suzanne, tell me what is going on. How can I help you if you don't tell me the problem?"

She wiped her tears with her red bandana, still sobbing. I tried to figure out what could have gone wrong. Nothing came into my head. Then suddenly she murmured, "My period..."

I was clueless. I watched her face, expecting a few more words from her. But again, she kept quiet. So I asked her, "Suzanne, what happened? What are you trying to tell me? Tell me everything clearly so that I will be able to do something to help you."

Her left toe was scratching the ground. Tears were coming down from her eyes. She was wiping her eyes. Her face was so red, it seemed she had been crying all night. Probably she did not know how to start. I guess she was searching for some words to explain what had happened. Finally, she opened her mouth and told me that her menstruation had been due two weeks before. She was afraid she was pregnant.

I couldn't believe my ears. I didn't know how to react. I just stared at her face. She was still looking down. She was still scratching the ground, with both hands covering her face. It was a total culture shock for me. No Nepali woman would have dared to say these things to a Nepali man, especially her supervisor. This would be taboo in Nepali culture. A Nepali girl would have refused to talk to me but would have confided in a trusted woman. I have heard of Nepali girls committing suicide, not being able to talk about their pregnancy with their friends and family and then not being able to abort the pregnancy. I admired the guts of American people for their ability to share and express their feelings and problems with their coworkers and supervisors.

After hearing her story, I slowly gathered my thoughts and advised her to go to Kathmandu to see the Peace Corps doctor. The next morning, I went to the school and told the headmaster that Suzanne had to go to Kathmandu for medical reasons. I lied and told them that I didn't know what was wrong with her. I told them that Americans are very particular about medical confidentiality and that our office regulations prohibited me from asking her any questions about medical issues, that only medical personnel had the authority to talk with patients about medical problems. I explained about medical leave and told them she would be back as soon as the doctor released her. We arranged for substitute teachers for her classes until she came back from Kathmandu.

My job required me to be a diplomat, and this meant I had to be able keep some information confidential and lie when needed. It was not the first time I had to keep confidential information from a headmaster about a volunteer's medical issues. On our way back to Kathmandu, Suzanne told me about Mike's visit to her village.

Ke Garne, Arnie?

Dr. Arnie, the Peace Corps physician, and I had an early morning flight from Kathmandu to Bhojpur, but as usual, the Royal Nepal Airlines Corporation (RNAC—known among the volunteers as Royal Nepal Airline Cancellation) flight was late and did not take off until noon. RNAC blamed the delay on the weather of Bhojpur airport, but we thought maybe a more lucrative mountain flight for tourists had taken precedence. We had left-side seats, hoping to get a good view of the mountains, but the sky was hazy and the mountains were not visible. The flight was bumpy, and we were scared out of our wits. Sometimes it felt like the plane was diving straight down at high speed. We landed at Bhojpur airport, a STOL (short takeoff and landing) airport serving people from Bhojpur and surrounding districts. The airport had been carved out of the side of the mountain below Taksar Bazaar. We collected our baggage and started walking up the hill toward Bhojpur Bazaar. It was normally a thirty-minute walk for me, but with Dr. Arnie, it took more than one hour. Maybe it took a little longer because both of us had heavy packs. It was a straight uphill walk to Taksar and then to Bhojpur Bazaar.

Arnie had joined me on this trip to visit volunteers in Bhojpur district because the medical staff were trying to visit as many volunteers as possible. We program officers were asked to share our volunteer visit schedule with the medical office a few weeks in advance so that they could tag along on the trip if possible. I was going to visit a total of three education volunteers in the district.

It was almost 2:00 p.m. when we got to Bhojpur Bazaar. We found a small bhat shop where the lady agreed to cook for us even though it was late to eat morning dal bhat and too early for evening dal bhat. Arnie had been in Nepal for almost a year but had never traveled outside Kathmandu Valley. He had not seen the volunteers' living situation in the villages and did not understand how much volunteers have to compromise in their daily life. While the food was cooking, we talked about water systems, potable water, the lack of foods Americans are used to, and other compromises volunteers had to make in their daily life.

When the lady told us that the food was ready, I asked her to dry our plates and glasses before putting food on our plates and water in our glasses. A major health problem in Nepali villages is waterborne diseases. We had to be careful to make sure we did not get sick on trips to visit volunteers in remote areas where we would not be able to get medical help. The lady did not understand what I was talking about. The Nepali custom is to wash the plates with cold water to clean them before serving food. I took out my clean handkerchief and wiped the plates and glasses. We had our own water, so I told the lady that we didn't need any water. The tarkari was spicy. I don't know how many chilis she had put in it. Arnie hardly ate any food—this was his first meal outside of Kathmandu in a real village setting. After dal bhat, Arnie bought a packet of coconut biscuits and chewed one after another until he finished the whole packet.

Bhojpur district is situated in the middle hills, and Bhojpur Bazaar is the district headquarters, serving as an administrative and business center for the people from Bhojpur and surrounding districts. This district has many beautiful waterfalls, rivers, and lakes. Taksar is well known for its metal works. Taksar is famous for the production of bronze *karuwa* (vessels for drinking water) and other household utensils. The *Bhojpure khukuri* (Gorkha knife) is the best-known product of Bhojpur.

We started our journey immediately after we finished our meal. It was a strenuous three-hour walk up and down to Danwa from Bhojpur. We made it to Danwa before dark. Arnie was hungry and tired and was complaining about the walk. It was good for him to know how volunteers lived in their posts. He was facing the reality of volunteer life in Nepal. That was the main reason for the medical office to have all their staff go and visit volunteers—so they would understand the living conditions of the volunteers in the villages and also the trails between Kathmandu and their villages. Arnie had no idea about the true situation in Nepali hill villages.

After we got to Danwa, Arnie and I took turns talking to Joe. Arnie listened when I was talking to Joe, and I listened when he was talking. If there had been any medical confidentiality issues, I would have absented myself from the talk, but they were talking about general issues of volunteers' village life, so it was all right for me to be with them while they were talking. Joe was a difficult volunteer. He had lot of complaints about everything—the headmaster, his colleagues, his food, and his living situation. He also complained about not getting medical supplies in time. He had requested a tube of antifungal cream about six or seven weeks ago but had not received it yet. His main complaint was not getting any responses from the medical office.

The next day I went to observe Joe's classes. On several occasions he lost his temper when the students could not answer his questions—especially the girls, who were either too shy to speak or did not know the answers. He was trying his best to make the girls speak and participate in class but had no luck. The girls sat with heads down chewing on their shawls. Joe had rearranged the classroom, having all the girls in the class sit in the front row.

After he finished teaching, we sat down and shared feedback at the school tea shop. He was receptive to the suggestions that I gave him. I also talked with him about school administration rules and regulations and the role of headmaster in a typical Nepali school. Usually in a Nepali school, all the teachers are from the same village and may be related to the headmaster, so it's difficult for the headmaster to discipline them for small issues. The headmaster had already given me some hints about Joe's high-handedness in administrative issues, like his displeasure with teachers with irregular attendance and those who did not teach the full period. We discussed all these issues and came up with some understandings for the future.

Friday was a big day for the volunteers in Bhojpur. Volunteers from the surrounding area would meet in Bhojpur on Friday evening for tomba. They had a common dera in Bhojpur. They went back to their villages on Saturday afternoon so that they would not miss teaching on Sunday morning. They always waited anxiously for Friday. Nepali schools had a one-and-a-half-day weekend—a half day Friday and the whole day Saturday. All three of us went to Bhojpur that Friday. The headmaster knew that Joe went to Bhojpur every Friday, so he knew Joe would probably leave school after finishing his classes.

There were six volunteers in Bhojpur that evening (three education and three from other programs), including two from neighboring Sankhuwasabha district. Everybody was happy to meet their colleagues. They stayed late that night drinking tomba, but Arnie went to bed early complaining about stomach pains. It was nice to be able to see the volunteers mingling with each other and sharing their frustrations and their achievements. Those who received "care packages" from their parents and friends for their birthday or other occasions shared them with their friends.

Charambi was a long day's walk from Bhojpur. We decided to start our walk immediately after we ate our morning meal on Saturday. Arnie was having stomach problems and had to run into the jungle many times on our way to Charambi. He was complaining all along the trail about the poor food and sanitation and wasn't able to walk that well. John, who was assigned to a school in Dingla, went back to his village directly, as he was about a ten-hour walk from Bhojpur. The trail was downhill most of the way with a lot of loose rocks, which made the path slippery and treacherous. It took us—Arnie, Sunita, and me—six hours to get to Charambi that day. Sunita, an American volunteer of Indian origin in her midthirties, was posted in the Charambi high school to teach mathematics and science.

I had discussed most of Sunita's issues with her while we were walking to Charambi, so when we got to Charambi, there was not much remaining to find out about her situation. Arnie was tired and did not even eat his meal. He went to sleep as soon as he got to Sunita's dera.

Sunday was a typical volunteer visit day. I went to observe Sunita's classes and sat down with her to discuss her teaching and to share ideas about teaching techniques appropriate for a Nepali school. I then spent some time with the headmaster and other teachers of the school. Sunita was doing well, and all the teachers and students liked her. She was a good teacher. She had taught in a school in a ghetto (disadvantaged ethnic minority or poor neighborhood) in New York city before she signed up to come to Nepal. Sunita had a Nepali *bahini* (sister), Rama, who was living with her in her dera. Rama was from a poor family and could not have continued her schooling if Sunita had not helped her. She cooked for Sunita and washed her clothes. In return, Sunita took care of Rama's expenses, including food, clothes, books, stationery, and school fees. Both of them were happy with the arrangement.

Arnie was sick and was tired from his walk. He didn't spend much time with the volunteers. He spent almost the whole day reading a paperback. In the evening, he spent some time with Sunita talking about medical issues.

As we had a long day ahead of us, we decided to start early in the morning. Arnie was not feeling well and could not carry his backpack, so we asked the headmaster to send the school office helper with us to Dingla. Around the middle of the day, we were tired and hungry. There were no bhat shops on the trail. The office helper took us to a village and asked a lady in a house if she could cook some food for us. She was hesitant, saying she did not have rice and vegetables suitable for *thu-*

lo manches ("big" or important people) from Kathmandu. We had to explain that we were used to traveling in Nepali villages and whatever she could make would be good for us. We rested while waiting for the food. Arnie had a good nap.

After we ate, I tried to pay the lady, but she would not accept any money. She said guests were like gods and that they never took any money for food from guests. Luckily, I had some pencils and notebooks with me, which I always carried for this kind of situation. I gave some of those school supplies to her daughter, who studied in a nearby primary school.

When we got to Dingla, the first thing I noticed was that John was lying on his bed. Arnie lay down on the *gundri* (straw mat) next to John's bed. Probably from the food he had eaten in Bhojpur, John had diarrhea and had to run to the *charpi* (outhouse) several times that day. He was also having bad cramps from time to time. John was happy to have the doctor there, but to our surprise Arnie was not ready to listen to John at all. Whenever John asked a question, he would say, "*Ke garne?* (What to do?) I'm sick too." For every question John asked him, he had the same readymade answer: "*Ke garne?* I'm sick too." Poor John had to live with his diarrhea and cramps for the whole night even though he had a doctor at his bedside. The next morning, he was feeling a little better, so we felt all right leaving him at his post.

The story of Arnie traveled among the volunteers so quickly that when we got to Kathmandu, they were already talking about Ke Garne Arnie's trip to Bhojpur. After that, volunteers simply started calling him Ke Garne Arnie instead of Dr. Arnie.

Don't Do That!

I grabbed his arm and told him to drop the hypodermic needle that he had just picked up from the floor and was attempting to put on the syringe. "Don't do that!" He looked puzzled but did not argue. He was a community health worker assigned to the health post in Libang, the district center of Rolpa district. He was at our volunteer Mike's dera trying to give him intravenous (IV) therapy for dehydration. Our Peace Corps nurse practitioner had flown in with me and could take over. The nurse practitioner had considerable experience and education and often filled in as medical officer when the physician was out of town. I thanked the community health worker, and he left.

According to the wireless message the medical office had received from Mike, he had a headache, lethargy, high fever, vomiting, and diarrhea. He had also mentioned that he was feeling weak and had occasional muscle cramps. The medical office was worried that these symptoms could possibly be life threatening.

Up to 60 percent of the human body is made up of water. Dehydration is the result of excessive loss of body fluid, losing more fluid than you take in, so your body doesn't have enough water to carry out its normal functions. Not replenishing lost fluid may cause serious consequences. Dehydration may happen because of heat exposure, prolonged and vigorous exercise, not drinking enough water, and some disease of the gastrointestinal tract. As the saying goes, "Prevention is better than cure." The best way to deal with dehydration is to prevent it from occurring. The treatment is fluid replacement. If the patient can take liquids orally, that is preferred, if not, then IV therapy is indicated.

Mike did not know how it happened, but all of a sudden, he had started getting stomach cramps and diarrhea. He told us that he was drinking water to prevent dehydration, but his symptoms persisted.

As per the medical office's request, we had chartered a helicopter to bring him to Kathmandu for treatment. The medical office requested that I accompany the pilot, as he was not sure that he would be able to find the cornfield near Mike's dera, even with the map and coordinates I had given him.

We had obtained permission from the chief district officer (CDO) to land in the cornfield, promising that Peace Corps would pay the field owner for damage caused by the helicopter. The CDO had requested the health worker to go and help the volunteer in any way he could. Our nurse practitioner was happy that the health worker had used proper judgment in providing him with dextrose solution by IV but I was upset with his carelessness. How could a medical worker pick up a needle from the floor and try to insert into a person's body? Was it just carelessness or ignorance?

Mike felt somewhat better with the fluids, but we decided to take him to Kathmandu, as we had the helicopter. There was another volunteer visiting Mike who was also not feeling well. The pilot decided to leave two jerry cans of fuel behind to reduce the weight and accommodate all five of us in the chopper. He told us that he would need to refill in Bhairahawa on our way to Kathmandu.

I learned that day how an educated and experienced person can make a mistake. I still wonder how the community health worker felt that day when I held his arm and prevented him from inserting the needle into Mike's vein.

Landing in the Middle of the Confluence

After flying for half an hour, the pilot contacted the tower in Bhairaha-wa to find out the weather situation. Rather than granting permission to land at Bhairahawa, the air traffic controller asked him to divert the helicopter toward Nepalgunj because of strong winds around Bhaira-hawa airport. He headed to Nepalgunj but got the same answer from the air traffic controller there. He could not figure out where to go.

All of a sudden, we felt the helicopter going down, shaking vi-olently. It seemed like the pilot had lost control. He looked around. Then I realized that he was looking for a place to land and wait for the weather to improve. He also wanted to save fuel, as leaving fuel in Libang had left him without any reserves. He saw a small island in the Rapti River. He landed the helicopter in a small clearing in the middle of the jungle on this tiny island with two sick volunteers. Luckily, Mike was feeling much better by that time, so we didn't have to worry much about him. We had never really worried about the other volunteer, as he was not that ill. Still, we felt very vulnerable on that island.

Evacuating a volunteer

A small rivulet joined the Rapti River several hundred meters above this island, split into two channels that again united below the island. The river was carrying trees and debris, anything that got in its way. The Rapti River and the rivulet had burst their banks. We felt like Robinson Crusoe—with the modern amenity of a flying machine, yet we felt stranded. We were in a dense forest in midmonsoon. The winds became so strong we didn't dare come out of the helicopter. We remained inside the full three hours we were there.

Our pilot finally heard that the weather in Bhairahawa area was improving, so he prepared to take off. We were relieved! It was already 5:30 p.m. when we landed at Bhairahawa. The pilot said he couldn't go to Kathmandu that day, as it was not permissible to land after 6:00 p.m. because there was no lighting at the airport. We had to spend the night in a hotel in Bhairahawa with two sick volunteers, but we had our nurse practitioner with us, so I wasn't worried. In spite of all our challenges, we were lucky to have a seasoned pilot who could land on that small island in the middle of a dense forest. I remember that situation sometimes and wonder how he managed to get down to that small clearing through the branches of those big, tall trees.

We made it to Kathmandu the next day and were happy that the trip had ended on a positive note in spite of our adventures. I heard later from the nurse practitioner that both volunteers had fully recovered and had been cleared to return to their posts.

Your Nephew is Already Dead

"Rhonda fell from the window of her house. She was unconscious for several minutes. Now she is talking but in severe pain. She may have broken her collarbone, as the local health assistant suggests. Or she could have other internal injuries. She is on pain killers. Please advise."

The above was a wireless message from a volunteer, Charlie, who was posted next to Rhonda's village. The headmaster had sent for Charlie as soon as he found out about Rhonda. I learned that this had happened in the early morning when it was still dark. Rhonda had gotten up to use the outhouse but went in the wrong direction and fell out the window, thinking it was a door.

The medical office received the message around 10:00 a.m. and informed me immediately, as Rhonda was my volunteer, and I was also the duty officer that week. The Peace Corps medical officer came to see me as soon as he got the message. We decided to charter a helicopter to evacuate her to Kathmandu.

As duty officer, it was my responsibility to arrange for the helicopter. I started by calling Colonel Basnet, the in-charge of the helicopter charter section. He told me he was unable to provide us with a helicopter that day, as all four helicopters had already been assigned to different flights. My only option was to get one from a private airline. I could not get hold of any of the private helicopter services by phone, so I drove to the airport hoping to meet someone and finalize the flight as soon as possible.

After I got to the airport, it took me several minutes to find Mr. Manandhar, who was in charge of one of the private helicopter services. When I walked into his office, he was about to leave. When I told him that I had serious business and I needed to talk to him, he was not interested. When I persisted, he impatiently said that his nephew had died and that people had gathered at Pashupati for the cremation. He also said that there was nobody who could arrange for a helicopter besides him, but he must go to Pashupati right away, and we would have to wait until tomorrow.

I was so upset with his behavior that I told him in a harsh voice, "Mr. Manandhar, your nephew has already died. You are going to participate in his cremation. He is not going to wake up from the funeral pyre because of your visit. There is nothing more you can do. He is dead. My volunteer is still alive. If we don't arrange the helicopter at this moment, she might die. What is more important for you? To save a dying person or to participate in the cremation of someone who has already died?"

His face changed. He looked at my face but did not speak. After a while he picked up the phone, dialed a number, and explained that there was an emergency and that he would go to Pashupati after taking care of this business. He then called two or three different pilots and arranged a flight for that afternoon. I flew in the helicopter to Rhonda's post. She had been taking painkillers and felt somewhat better. We were able to bring her to Kathmandu that evening. A Peace Corps vehicle was waiting for us at the airport. We immediately took her to the medical office, and the medical office took care of the situation after that.

Sometimes you have to go out of your comfort zone to be heard.

An Altered Reality

Mr. Jung Shah, the headmaster of Rob's school, and I had a long discussion about Rob's teaching, his activities, his secondary project, and teacher training. The headmaster told me that everybody liked Rob's way of teaching science. He never went to his classroom without some practical work or experiment for the students to do. Like the Nepali teachers, he did not have expensive science equipment. Rob used only low-cost or no-cost materials, whereas it seemed that the lack of science equipment prevented the Nepali teachers from doing any experiments. Other science teachers in the area had heard about Rob's innovativeness, and they had been requesting him to run a training program on the preparation of science teaching materials.

I went for the inauguration of Rob's training and also to visit some other volunteers in the area. The headmaster was happy with Rob's activities at the school and the small projects he was conducting in the village. The headmaster wanted to take the opportunity of Rob's teacher training to let his school's name shine in the locality. Rob had been designing his training sessions and preparing examples of science equipment made from locally available materials. It looked like he was very comfortable with what he was planning to do. He was also using his counterpart Nepali teacher, Binod Bhatta, as a cotrainer. The two of them were a strong team, with Binod supporting Rob in the Nepali language and Rob supporting Binod in the creation of innovative materials.

Mr. Shah had invited officials from the district headquarters for the inauguration ceremony. Rob did not like the idea of making his training a big show, as it was just a few days' basic training, but the headmaster did not want to lose a chance to show off in front of the local government officials and political leaders. Mr. Shah invited the CDO and the district education officer (DEO) of Bajhang District and other office heads. Both the CDO and the DEO did attend the inauguration of the training. Everything went as planned. Rob ran the first session, how to make a scale from a ballpoint pen. He showed how to use the spring of a pen to appropriately calibrate the scale by hanging known weights from the spring. He marked the outside of the pen when each successive weight was added. The participants were encouraged to follow along with materials provided to them. There were many other such exercises.

Certainly, Peace Corps language training was not sufficient to instruct in this kind of activity. Peace Corps volunteers had only three months of language training—just survival language, but not enough technical language to run a teacher training session. I noticed that Rob was able to be as creative with language as he was with the materials he created. He used English technical words and ended sentences with Nepali verb endings. That is similar to how educated Nepali people show off their mastery of English language. People were impressed with his presentation and demonstrations. The trainees as well as the observers enjoyed the class.

After the training was over that first day, the dignitaries from the district headquarters left. We did not know that the headmaster had a big plan for the night. He had requested the CDO and the DEO to stay, but they declined, saying they had busy schedules the next day. After the CDO and the DEO left, the headmaster and the teachers killed a goat and prepared for the party. We had plenty of meat and drinks. Everybody ate and drank their fill and enjoyed the party. Then a local *deuda* dance program was presented in which everybody stood in a circle and moved their feet a step forward and a step backward. The local people were singing in their dialect, so we were not able to understand the songs.

Drink was flowing. After being in the circle for about fifteen or twenty minutes, I noticed someone lighting a cigarette. He took one or two puffs and then passed the cigarette to the person on his left. I had a hard time understanding why nobody had more than one or two puffs. When it came to me, I tried to pass, as I had not smoked for the last fifteen years, but they would not listen. I had no choice but take a puff. After a few minutes, I felt dizzy and nauseated. I did not know what was happening to me, but I didn't want to disappoint the others by leaving.

After a while my feet were not strong enough to be able to keep me standing up. I was stumbling, unable to walk properly. Somehow, I managed to tell the headmaster that I had to go. I think Rob noticed my behavior, and when he saw me talking to the headmaster, he came to my rescue. He took me to his room and took out my sleeping bag for me. I lay down in my sleeping bag, but I could not sleep. Rob went back to the party. I felt spaced out and a little drunk. I could see the ceiling revolving. I felt like I was dreaming, but when I pinched my wrist, I realized I was not.

Different thoughts came and went. The house itself was swaying back and forth as if a very strong earthquake had just hit the area. I remember getting my water bottle and drinking water several times. I was lost. I did not know what I was doing. I could not remember in what language I was thinking, if I was thinking anything at all. It was the most tormented hours of my life, in a place where I knew very few people. Now I realized why they were not having more than one puff. I did not know what would have happened to me if I had taken more than one. I don't remember how long I stayed awake. I felt sick, and I had nausea. I had no idea what was going on. If I had known that they had hash in those cigarettes, I would have never tried them. Even though it happened unknowingly, it was an experience of altered reality due to being *ganja lagyo* (high on hashish) and *rakshi lagyo* (drunk). I would not want to repeat this ever again in my life. One time was enough.

The next day Rob explained that local people often put hashish in their cigarettes. They would take out some tobacco from the cigarette, put a small amount of hashish in, and then put back the tobacco. Rob knew this custom, so he was able to avoid it. Later he told me that alcohol and pot together can give a very strong reaction. As he knew that I didn't smoke, he did not even think about warning me. It was my first and last experience with hashish.

I was still not feeling very energetic the next morning. I was even hesitant to go to observe classes, as I was sure some participant must have noticed my condition the night before. I did go to observe two more sessions, one session conducted by Rob and the other by Binod. They stood side by side in each session to help each other whenever needed. I saw them working very well as a team. That was one of our aims in these trainings: transfer of skills. The motto was to train the counterpart to do the job after the volunteer completed their term of assignment.

That afternoon after the training, Rob and I took a walk along the bank of the Seti River. On that walk he explained how the local people would go up in the mountains where marijuana grew wild. People would spend the whole day in the jungle, rubbing marijuana leaves in their palms to extract a glue-like substance that was much more powerful than marijuana. After they rubbed the marijuana plant in their hands, the resin on their hands would be several millimeters thick. They would then make round balls out of it—this was hashish. That was a side income for the local people, as there was good demand for it in Kathmandu and other cities. Every member of the local households became involved, as it was a source of extra income for them.

By the evening I was feeling normal again. Rob and I talked more about the training, and I thanked the headmaster for being so helpful in arranging the logistics for the training. The headmaster was happy with the outcome of the training. He was especially happy about the presence of the CDO and DEO in his village, which made him a hero in the village.

Life Hanging on a Rope

The next morning, I started the seven- or eight-hour walk from Chain-pur, Rob's post, to Thalara. We had our dal bhat early, around 9:00 a.m. Rob went to continue his teacher training immediately after eating, and I started my trip to Thalara. There were a few people on the trail, mainly going south to the big border towns to get their supply of salt and kerosene for the coming monsoon months. Men wore *daura sururwal*, and women wore *ghangar* (a long skirt made of five or six meters of cloth, gathered at the waist). By midday, the summer sun had scorched the ground as if it was trying to evaporate every drop of moisture from everything that it could possibly come in contact with. A cool breeze would have made my life easier, but that was just a daydream.

Thalara is not a very well-known destination, even in the midwestern region. In earlier times there was a large settlement in that area. The ruins of ancient buildings were still visible. We could still see the remains of an old castle and stone pillars with some inscriptions. The engraved letters on those pillars were difficult to discern, as the sun and rain had worn down the letters in most places.

Cattle and hashish were the main cash crops of Thalara. Even though they raised cattle, milk was forbidden to be sold in the local tea shops because of a taboo. The local superstition was that the cow or water buffalo that provided the milk would get sick or even die if anybody from an untouchable caste happened to drink its milk. They produced *ghee* (purified butter) from milk and took the ghee to big bazaars for sale. Instead of fresh milk, they use Amul, the Indian powdered milk.

A custom I found out about while talking to the people on the trail was that during menstruation cycle, women had to spend their days in a cowshed, known as the practice of *chhaupadi*. I heard of women losing their lives because of the poor hygiene and cold that they had to experience in these cowsheds. Women had to live in the cowshed also while giving birth, up until the baby's naming ceremony, which happens on the twelfth or thirteenth day. During their period and after childbirth, the women can't touch any food or water that will be consumed by others. Men can't go near them. This is a very strong custom in the westernmost hill districts of Nepal, and it was especially difficult for the female volunteers. Nepal's government has been trying to banish this custom but has had little success. It is difficult to find a compromise that keeps both parties happy while also trying to change for the betterment of individuals and the society as a whole.

Another strange custom that is still prevalent in the area is the *deuki* system. There are temples in the area where local people promise the gods or the goddesses that they will offer certain things if their problems are resolved. For example, a wealthy family may promise to offer a deuki if a sick family member gets well. Offering deuki means buying a young girl from a poor family and offering that girl to take care of the temple. When the girl grows up, the cash offerings in the temple are not sufficient to support her life, so she often will become a prostitute. Even now, deuki can be seen in some of the temples of this area, not that much in Bajhang but more in Dadeldhura, Baitadi, and Darchula areas.

It was around 4:30 p.m. when I got to a place called Simle. I was confused because I did not see any sign of a trail from there. Luckily, a man arrived just a few minutes after I got there. He explained that I had to either cross the Seti River with the help of a rope or walk another three hours where there was a bridge to cross the river. He told me he was going to cross the river right there. I decided to wait and see how he did it. Here I was in a dilemma, because I had been telling volunteers not to walk at night for their personal safety, and I myself was now forced either to walk for three hours in the dark or to cross the river with the help of a rope.

I was looking at the man crossing the river. A long *babiyo* (a kind of grass) rope was tied to trees on both sides of the river. The rope was about two inches in diameter. Part of a tree branch was hooked over the rope, and the lower part of the branch formed an inverted T shape, which was used as a seat. A thinner rope was tied to that crude seat and was attached to trees on both sides of the river. I saw the man holding the thinner rope with one hand and pulling it, which made him slide toward the other bank of the river. It took him about ten minutes to cross the river. I looked down. The river was swollen, gushing with high-speed blue mountain water.

Now I had to decide what I wanted to do. Do I want to cross the river with the help of the rope, or do I want to walk another three hours to get to the bridge? From the bridge it would take another hour to get to Thalara. The man was gone. He had crossed the river and started walking, as it was not a big deal for him. He probably crossed here every day.

I sat on a stone nearby, unable to decide what to do. Different thoughts came into my mind. What if the rope broke? What if my hands slipped? I did not have much time, as it was going to get dark soon. I finally said to myself if he can do it, I could too. I walked toward the river. I pulled the piece of wood by pulling the thinner rope. I had a backpack with about fifteen pounds of supplies on my back. I held that piece of rope and wood and started pulling the thinner rope. I wanted to close my eyes, but I could not do that because I needed to know when I reached the other side of the river. I knew I was risking my life. I turned around and sat on the same stone again where I was sitting before. While I was debating with myself, another person came and crossed the river, as it was not really a big deal for these people. I spent more than half hour not being able to decide what to do. Again, I went to the place to cross the river. This time, I just sat on that piece of wood and started pulling the thinner rope to take me to the other side of the river. I could not look down. The gushing sound of the river was earsplitting. I could not put my hands on my ears, as both of my hands were busy holding the thinner rope and the seat. All of sudden my pack felt very heavy, and I was having a problem balancing it. It felt lopsided, as if it was going to pull me down into the river, but I could not do anything to balance the weight.

It felt like it took me fifteen hours, not fifteen minutes, to cross that river. It took all my courage. I don't know how many people had died trying to cross the Seti River here with the help of that rope. It was the most alarming and dangerous adventure I had ever faced in my life. I hoped I would not have to do it again.

Panikhala

It was one of those long field trips about which Kamala used to tease me, saying, "When you come back, I will have the divorce papers ready." Some of my friends would ask me, "Do your daughters recognize you when you come back from your field trips?" Some of these trips were three or four weeks long, several days' drive and several days' walk. Or if we were lucky, sometimes we were able to start from Kathmandu in a small Pilatus Porter or Twin Otter plane. Sometimes I did worry that my daughters really might not recognize me when I came back from these long trips, filthy, not having showered or shaved for many days.

But I was not ready to quit my job, because I was getting the utmost satisfaction from all my duties. I kept reminding myself that we provided assistance to those poor, remote village schools, without any financial burden to the government of Nepal. I had been lucky enough to be able to work for the Peace Corps where one of my major responsibilities was to select schools for posting education volunteers. The volunteers taught for one year and conducted teacher training the next year. The lack of qualified subject teachers was a major problem in most of these schools, and Peace Corps volunteer teachers were a godsent gift for those schools.

We had a policy of posting volunteers mainly in remote areas, as we saw more need in those villages. This made our volunteer visit trips difficult and even dangerous at times. But if an American volunteer could spend two years of their valuable time in one of our remote villages, why should I hesitate to visit them once a year? My issue was that I had about sixty volunteers at a time (about thirty in their first year and thirty in their second year), and I needed to visit all of them within a year. I had to visit all thirty of those in their first year at least once. If they had any problems, I might have to visit them several times. The volunteers were scattered throughout the remote districts such as Darchula, Baitadi, Dadeldhura, Bajhang, Achham, Jumla, Humla, Kalikot, Rukum, Taplejung, Panchthar, Sankhuwasabha, and Solukhumbu.

This trip was to visit a total of thirteen volunteers, five in Baitadi, two in Darchula and three in Dadeldhura, then others in Doti and Bajhang. We drove all the way to Jhulaghat, which took us about three days, then crossed the border and walked uphill to Gothalapani, the headquarters of Baitadi district. I then went to Doti to visit volunteers in Uchchakot, Kalukheti, Dipayal, and Silgadhi. We divided our work. My colleagues visited some of these volunteers, and I visited some of them. After completing our work in Doti, I decided to go to Bajhang, and my colleagues flew back to Kathmandu from Dipayal.

Not knowing the trail and also having a large load with mail and gift packages for volunteers, I decided to hire a porter from Silgadhi to Bajhang. Even with the porter, my backpack weighted about twenty-five pounds, which was a lot of weight for me. We started early to make it to Panikhala village before nightfall. We had *puri-tarkari* (fried bread with curry) for breakfast in Silgadhi and hit the road after that. The trail was very remote, no tea shops and no trekkers. We hardly saw anybody that whole day.

Around 2:00 p.m., it started getting cloudy and dark. We had started feeling moisture in the air, and it was cold. We must have been at about six thousand feet. The trail kept disappearing into the thick forest. All of a sudden, we were hit by hailstones. The hail was almost as big as table tennis balls, and it was painful when we got hit. There were no houses nearby to take shelter. We got drenched in rain, and it became difficult to walk. We stopped underneath a big tree for a while. Then the porter told me there were some houses a few minutes down below our trail. We walked about half an hour and came to a house. The porter called out and banged on the door. Finally, a lady opened the door. The porter told her our problem and asked if we could spend the night in her house. He was talking to her because I did not know the local dialect. Later, the porter explained that the lady would not let us stay even on the *pindhi* of the house, as there were no male family members at home.

We had no choice but to continue to another nearby house. By this time, I was so tired, I could not wait for the porter to talk with the owner of the house. I just put my backpack on the *pindhi*, changed into dry clothes, and got in my sleeping bag to escape the bitter cold. It took me a few minutes to get warm enough to be able to think straight. I remained in my sleeping bag for some time and slowly emerged.

I saw my porter at one corner of *pindhi* making *roti*. He had a fire going, and he was kneading dough. I went to sit near the fire. He already had two or three *rotis* made. The porter had talked to the owner of the house and gotten approval for us to spend the night in his house. The rotis were thick, and probably the inside was not cooked well. I did not know when the porter had last washed his hands. His hands had dirt smeared all over them. He offered me two rotis. I just could not think of eating those rotis. I thanked him, and I went back to my sleeping bag and slept. I did not want to get sick on the trail.

We woke up early the next morning and started our walk. The trail was downhill all the way to Panikhala. It was slippery and treacherous from the previous night's rain and hail. The sun was shining on the other side of the valley, but the trail on our side was still muddy as the sun had not reached our side. We were walking toward the west, and the sun slowly started warming our backs. It took us about five hours to get to Panikhala. As there were no tea shops in the village, the porter took me to the *pradhan panch*'s (the village mayor's) house. I met the pradhan panch and told him about my trip. When we got to his house, we noticed that his wife had already prepared his morning meal. After our short conversation, he insisted that I sit down on the *pirka* (a low wooden seat) and asked me to eat the food prepared for him. I felt uneasy but could not avoid it, as he was showing respect, and I was also very hungry. It was a very unpleasant-looking dish. It was parboiled (*ushina chaamal ko bhaat*) rice with *shisnu tarkari* (greens made of stinging nettles) on top of it. Not very appetizing, but that was not an unusual meal for that part of the country, if you were lucky enough to eat. I ate two or three morsels and could not eat more than that. I could not say I didn't want to eat, because the pradhan panch of the village had given me the food that he was ready to eat with utmost respect. But there was no way I could have eaten more than I already had. So, I made an excuse that I had severe stomach pain and left the food. I felt really bad about it, as food was very scarce in that part of the country, and I was still very hungry.

I stood up holding my stomach and slowly went to wash my hands. Then I took out my sleeping bag and lay down for a while. About an hour later, I told them that I was feeling a little better and prepared to go. I tried to pay for the food, but the pradhan panch would not take any money from me. I took out a few notebooks and pencils from my backpack and handed them over to the kids playing outside in the verandah. After that I took leave from him and started walking toward Kalukheti.

After walking for a while, I was so hungry that I stopped and took out the last package of Nebico biscuit, (a pioneer biscuit industry of Nepal) from my backpack. The porter had eaten well both the night before and this morning. It was interesting to see that the local people seemed healthy despite the food they ate. Hygiene is not a big problem for them. It may be because they develop a strong immune system from childhood.

The hills of the Far Western and Midwestern Development Regions (currently State numbers 6 and 7) have low literacy, are underdeveloped, and are notorious for having poor hygiene. I have great respect for the volunteers who have changed the lives of villagers by teaching them good hygiene and good food habits. Surprisingly enough, most volunteers adapt well to Nepali culture and the surrounding environment. Their willingness to teach what they know to the villagers is praiseworthy. There can't be any comparison between their lives back home in America and their village life in Nepal. Most of the volunteers eat two meals of *dal bhat* and have only popcorn for snacks throughout their whole two years in Nepal. Being able to adapt is one of the signs of a successful volunteer.

It took us about six hours to get to Kalukheti, my next destination. Bill had been at the post for the last six months. We had communicated through Nepali mail, which took about two weeks each way between Kathmandu and Kalukheti. Talking to Bill and his coworkers and the headmaster, it seemed he was doing his mathematics and science teaching job well. It was a very new experience for him, and it was a culturally difficult post. It was also a very remote post. Food was scarce. No packaged food was available there except some Nepali biscuits. He had to fly from Kathmandu or from Nepalganj to Bajhang airport and walk all day to get to his post. I had taken another route on this trip, as I was in the neighboring district, Doti. So it took me a little longer to walk to Kalukheti from Silgadhi. My porter was carrying several weeks of Bill's mail. The Kathmandu office sent volunteers mail once a week, but as I was planning to visit him, they had his mail on hold to send with me. My porter also carried Bill's care packets from home and some food I was bringing for him such as peanut butter, Nescafe, granola, and chocolates.

Bill was very happy to see me and went crazy when he saw all his packages. He asked me to excuse him and started opening his mail. It was like Christmas for him. We then talked about his situation in Kalukheti. We discussed his health, his teaching and related problems, cultural issues, the food situation, and language. Language was a problem because people there spoke their own local dialect. While we were talking, he started preparing dinner for the night. He made a very good meal of noodles and salad. He had a small kitchen garden where he grew his own vegetables. The salad was from his own garden. Somehow, he had a good collection of all the ingredients needed for different dishes. He also made some roti and veggies. The roti was much better than what the porter had made the night before. He proved himself a very good cook. Boiled and filtered water and tasty food! What more could I have asked for?

A Murder Mystery

Phil Cyr was a dedicated Peace Corps volunteer with a lot of enthusiasm. A graduate of the University of Connecticut, he was working as a true emissary of John F. Kennedy. Even now he is still well remembered by his colleagues and his students. He was posted at Mukti High School, in Ratamata in Pyuthan district. He was dedicated to his work, very punctual, and regular in his duty at the school. The headmaster was very happy with his work.

Sometime in October 1980, I received a letter from Phil briefing me about a trip he had planned to Dhorpatan. I was his program officer, so he had to keep me informed of his whereabouts. He told me how amazed he had been by the view of the Dhaulagiri range on his last trip, when he had gone just halfway to Dhorpatan. This time he wanted to go all the way to Dhorpatan during Dashain vacation. He also wrote that he had only twenty rupees left, so he was going to sell his tape recorder to have enough money for food and also to hire a porter or guide, as he was new in the area. This happened to be my last communication with him.

He left his school for this trip when the Dashain vacation started and was planning to return a few days before school started. After Dashain I assumed that he was already back at school, as he was punctual and dedicated to his job. His headmaster told me that Phil had not missed a single day of teaching since he was assigned to the school in January. I was surprised to get a letter from the headmaster two weeks after the Dashain vacation saying that he was worried about Phil, as he had not shown up at school. He had written this a few days after school had resumed. He mentioned Phil's punctuality, his love for the students at the school, and his dedication to his job. He also wrote that Phil was never late returning to post. He always arrived a day early to prepare for his classes. He sounded worried that something bad must have happened to Phil or that he might be somewhere where no communication was available. I shared the letter with the country director, and we immediately began to take action.

I sent wireless messages to all the district education offices in the area asking them if they had seen or met Phil Cyr, an American volunteer traveling in that area. Another possibility we thought of was that he could have decided to visit a fellow PCV and might have gotten sick while staying with them. Knowing Phil, this was unlikely, but we still sent messages to almost all the volunteers in the Western and Mid-Western regions.

We did not get any leads. Now we started worrying. The rule was that we must inform Peace Corps Washington within a certain time if a PCV was missing. We did not want to alarm them but did send a message saying that Phil had not reported to his post after the Dashain vacation. Now we started getting pressure from Washington to expedite our search. Phil's parents, Jean and Normand Cyr, had been informed, and we assured them that we were doing everything possible to find him. In the meantime, we chartered a Russian helicopter from the Nepal army with a capacity of about twenty passengers. We flew to Dhorpatan and divided into four groups. We combed all the area surrounding Dhorpatan but did not get any clues.

The Peace Corps announced a fifty-thousand-rupee reward to anyone who could give us information about Phil. Soon we were surprised to find out that a local woman had gone to the police office in Burtibang to report that her husband was involved in murdering Phil. There was a gang of three people, including the one who was his porter. They had a fight distributing Phil's money and belongings. The other two had threatened to kill her husband, so he absconded to India. With that information, the local police snatched the two conspirators, and they served a twenty-year jail term. Since the incident happened in 1981, they were to have been in jail until 2001.

After several months, Phil's parents decided to visit Nepal. We took them to his post and nearby areas. We also took them to Pokhara. One morning in Pokhara when we were having tea, I told them how sorry we were about what had happened to Phil. Phil's mother, Jean, was a kind and compassionate lady. I was touched to hear her say, "Ambika, it could have happened in my backyard in New York. There are good and bad people everywhere." I wondered if I could be this clear-headed if something similar had happened to one of my daughters. How can a mother who just lost her son express this kind of feeling?

From 1964 to 1998, ten volunteers died during their service in Nepal. There was also Nancy Hart, who disappeared a few months after her close of service (COS) on a trip to Kala Paththar, a trekkers' paradise in the region of Mount Everest. The news of missing PCVs started appearing in local and national newspapers in the US. The Peace Corps takes the volunteers' safety very seriously, but staff can only provide guidance and hope the volunteers heed our advice.

Hash Brownies

Somebody knocked on my hotel room door around 10:30 p.m. It was Shyam Shrestha, our general services assistant, who was in Pokhara helping me run the Western Regional Conference. It was the last day of the conference. We had about fifty volunteers from all over the Western region. Every year, Peace Corps / Nepal organizes conferences all over Nepal on a regional basis. We usually had four regional conferences as the Far-West and Mid-West had a joint conference.

The conferences were designed to help the volunteers in their technical fields and also to provide them support in culture and language. It was also a good venue to collect feedback from the volunteers. Volunteers looked at it as a time to meet their friends and air out their issues, problems, and grievances.

Shyam told me that there were two volunteers in one room who were seriously ill. He did not explain more. I went to their room and, seeing their condition, called the Peace Corps nurse who was also in Pokhara for the conference. The volunteers looked like they were in a waking dream, saying nonsensical words. When the nurse arrived, I left the room requesting her to keep me informed of the situation. As associate director, I was fully responsible for running the conference. The nurse contacted medical personnel in Pokhara for assistance. That night, the nurse came to see me and told me that it was a drug case. It was a case of ingesting too many hash brownies.

We heard that there were other volunteers who had also eaten the brownies but were not as much impacted. They may have known what was in them and so took fewer brownies. But the two sick volunteers were unaware of what was in the brownies and probably ate quite a few.

As it was late at night and the volunteers had been stabilized, we decided to meet with them the next morning. Drug cases are very serious in the Peace Corps. If we found someone abusing drugs, there was no recourse but to immediately administratively separate the volunteer and send him/her back to the US within twenty-four hours. They could appeal to Peace Corps / Washington, but the country director made the decision in-country. As conference in-charge, I had to report everything to the country director. But at that time, the country director was on vacation, and I was working as the acting country director. I had to make the decision.

Mark and Leslie were the two volunteers who were sick that night. They had been unaware that the brownies contained hashish. The nurse gave me the names of a few more volunteers who had eaten the brownies. The next morning, I prepared an interview schedule for all the volunteers who were involved. My plan had been to drive to Kathmandu early that morning, but I needed to deal with this issue immediately. I met with each of the ten volunteers one by one, and it took all day.

Two volunteers had brought hashish from Kathmandu and made the brownies at their dera. They prepared about fifty brownies and took them to the conference hall on the last day of the conference without telling anyone that the brownies contained hashish. Two additional volunteers were at Regina's apartment while they were baking the brownies, and they knew about the scheme and ate some of the brownies. After completing all the interviews, I told the four guilty volunteers to come to Kathmandu. I left for Kathmandu the next day.

Once I got to Kathmandu, I called for a senior staff meeting and discussed the incident. We decided not to wait until the country director came back from his vacation but to take action immediately. We thought it could leave a bad precedent for other volunteers if we didn't take immediate action. The medical office agreed with our decision and gave me a long report explaining the incident and the possible consequences of not intervening at this stage. Another program officer, Renee Thakali, helped me communicate with PC / Washington and gave me much moral support. I really needed and appreciated her support at that time.

Immediately after our staff meeting, I called the four volunteers and informed them of our decision. We gave them a week to go to their posts to collect their belongings and say goodbye to the people in their villages. We told them that the Pan Am award (a Pan American Airways plane ticket) would be waiting for them when they arrived in Kathmandu the next week.

They could not believe our decision; they were shocked. They assumed that they would just get a warning, as it was their first incident. They also thought we would not be able to make such a bold decision in the absence of the country director. They hoped that by the time the director came back from vacation, the case would fade into the background.

They questioned my authority to send them home, but I stood firm in our decision. One of the volunteers threatened me, saying that his father was a well-known lawyer in Washington, DC, who would not hesitate to take this case to court. I told them they could do whatever they wanted but that our decision was final and that there was no time to wait until the country director came back from vacation. In fact, I had already called the country director to explain about the incident and told him what we had decided to do. He fully agreed with us and gave us a green light to go ahead with our decision. To administratively separate four volunteers at one time was serious, and we felt sorry for them, but the situation demanded that we do it. All four volunteers left for America immediately after they arrived from their villages.

The same is the case with riding a motorcycle without a helmet. Several volunteers in other countries had died because of not wearing a helmet. The Peace Corps had developed strong regulations. The rule was that any volunteer driving or riding a motorcycle without a helmet would be terminated from service. We once had to send one of our Nepal volunteers home because of not wearing a helmet.

People eventually have to face up to the consequences of their actions.

The Conflict Begins

It was the month of June, and it was hot down in Chitawan. Usually monsoon season starts around the end of May, but there was no sign of rain even in mid-June this year. Chitawan did not have a good irrigation system in those days, and most of the farming depended on monsoon rain, which farmers were anxiously awaiting. On the dusty roads of Chitawan, I was driving from one school to another looking for possible posts for our new trainees arriving in September. We were expecting about thirty education volunteers. I had to find about fifteen more posts, which would make forty-five schools in total, to give the volunteers enough choices.

I was talking to Mr. Khan, the headmaster at the Adikabi High School in Narayan Ghat, when the accountant of the school came to the headmaster's room and told me that there was a phone call for me from Kathmandu. It was Tika Karki, the deputy director, asking me to return to Kathmandu immediately because a volunteer in Dang district was having problems. I needed to go immediately to Kathmandu and then to Dang to take care of it. I finished Adikabi's post survey. I liked the school and how committed the teachers and School Managing Committee members were to ensuring the school's excellence. The faculty was excited about the possibility of working with a volunteer. By the time I left the school, it was almost four o'clock; even then, I headed toward Kathmandu and got home around 9:00 p.m.

I went to see the director the next morning. He was upset, but I had a hard time finding out why. Finally, I learned that he had heard that the volunteer in Dang was abusing drugs and that he made frequent visits to Indian border towns to get his supplies. As I have already related, drug use was a big offense in Peace Corps, and a rumor from a reliable source was enough to early terminate (ET) the volunteer. There was nothing I could do from Kathmandu. I had to forget my post preparation work for a while and prepare for my trip to Dang to visit Dick. Dick had finished his year of teaching in a secondary school and had moved on to a teacher training role in the SEDU in Tulsipur, Dang, for his second year. The SMT was happy with his performance. The SMT had communicated with me that Dick was always willing to take an extra load when necessary. He always prepared his teaching materials ahead of time. The SMT had also told me that Dick loved to prepare low-cost/no-cost teaching materials and that he involved the teacher trainees in preparing these materials.

Monsoon is the worst season in Nepal to travel. Flights get canceled, and roads get blocked because of floods and landslides. Due to the uncertainty of flights, I decided to drive to Dang to visit with Dick. I started early from Kathmandu but only reached Butwal that day. I spent the night at the Butwal Technical Institute guest house. I made it to Dang around noon the next day. Luckily, there were not many landslides. This road was new, and the monsoon rains could have easily washed out the areas that had recently been filled in, triggering landslides up and down the road. Lots of excavation takes place to build roads in the hills. It takes time for the earthworks to settle.

Dick was surprised to see me. Usually the program officers would send our travel schedule to the volunteers a few weeks before a trip. But this was an unplanned trip, so there was no way to inform him.

I did not bring up the drug issue with him to start with, as I wanted to observe his work and behavior. I was hoping that I would come up with some clues by observation. I stayed with him for two days, observing his classes and providing feedback on his teacher training. We also talked about his health, living situation, and his relationships with his coworkers and trainees. I was with him all the time except when we went to bed and when I was talking to his supervisor, Mr. Mohan Basnet, the SMT. We talked about Dick's job performance, his interaction with the trainees, his adjustment to village life, and his lifestyle.

Mr. Basnet had no complaints, and he was very happy with Dick's job performance. Mr. Basnet told me that the trainees were happy to have Dick as one of their trainers. Dick was competent and had not missed any of his classes.

As I still had no clues about Dick's drug use and frequent trips to the Indian border, I was forced to ask him if he frequented Indian border towns for supplies. He said he had a multiple entry visa to go to India and that he went to the Indian border with his Nepali colleagues at the SEDU to purchase school supplies. Then I spent some time with Dick's colleagues. They were surprised when I asked them what they did in the border town. I also asked them how often they went and what they usually bought. They wondered why I was asking about their routine excursions. As I was not getting any clues, I decided to revisit the SMT. This time I told him the reason behind my trip and asked him if he had heard of or seen Dick using any kind of contraband drugs. Mohan was surprised and said he would never consider such a thing. Later, I also told Dick the reason for my trip and that the information seemed to be wrong. I had seen no sign that he was using drugs.

The third day, I drove back to Kathmandu, arriving late at night. The next day I went to see the director and told him my findings. I told him that Dick was doing a good job and that everybody, including his Nepali supervisor, his colleagues, and his trainees were happy with his work. The director did not accept my findings and asked me to prepare to ET Dick. I refused. We had a long discussion, and he tried to convince me that a volunteer could be early terminated if drug use information came from a reliable source, in this case the director himself. I did not want to ET him without proof, because it would remain on his record forever. I did not carry through with Dick's termination. The conflict between this director and me started from here and lasted until the director left Nepal many months later.

At one point I even tendered my resignation, as the situation got so out of control that it was hard for me to work under him. He did not accept my resignation, but those one and a half years were the most difficult of my whole thirty years of Peace Corps service. I realized that power can make people blind and that sometimes people try to use their power without looking at the long-term consequences.

I would have terminated Dick as I had others if I had any proof that he was using drugs. But my conscience did not allow me to, even though I had to disobey my supervisor and have a miserable and uncomfortable life for his remaining tenure in Nepal, long after this volunteer's case was settled.

The Harassment

"I am putting you on probation. I am giving you three months to improve your English," the country director told me one day when I went to see him.

"I have been in this job for more than two decades. Up until now nobody has questioned my ability to do my job. My evaluations by previous supervisors have been excellent until now. Why, all of a sudden, do I need to improve my English language now to do my job efficiently?"

I was shocked. This was after I had served in the Peace Corps for over two decades, about ten years as associate director and about ten years before that as a language trainer, administrative assistant, and general service assistant.

The country director was adamant. "I don't want to discuss it; you have to improve your English. That is all I know. The Peace Corps will pay for your language classes." It seemed as if he was trying to find an issue to harass me.

It was the first time in my professional life that I had faced such a situation. I always had cordial relationships with both supervisors and subordinates. In this very job, I had worked under eight other country directors, and everything had gone well until that point.

I went home and discussed it with Kamala. I called my daughters in America and told them what was going on. All three of them unanimously supported my resigning from my job if I was having such a hard time working with my supervisor. He had eighteen more months in Nepal. To work under these conditions for eighteen more months would not be easy. We had a long discussion. What was I going to do if my resignation got approved? How easy would it be for me to find another job in Kathmandu? I sat on the issue for several days. Would I be able to work with my current supervisor for another eighteenth months? What else could he do to make my life more miserable?

All this had happened on a Wednesday morning. I waited to face him until early Monday morning. I wrote my resignation, clearly indicating that I would not be able to work under the current situation. Verbally, I told him that I would work under him only if he withdrew my probation. How could I work effectively if my colleagues all knew the director disapproved of me?

After he read my resignation, I saw his face changing. He thrust the resignation paper to me and said, "Ambika, we can work together. You have worked in this institution for twenty years. I am not going to accept your resignation. Improving your language would be beneficial to you in the long run. Go to the American Language Center and enroll in an English-language class."

I noticed the change in his tone. I had no qualms about taking English-language classes. Everybody has room for improvement. English is my second language anyway, so I knew I could improve. It was not the language lessons that I was worried about. It was his attitude toward me. I felt insulted to be put on probation after all my hard work.

I had served the Peace Corps very loyally. There were times when people suspected Peace Corps volunteers and Peace Corps employees of being CIA agents. But I knew how the Peace Corps functioned and that there was a strong separation between the Peace Corps and the CIA and other US intelligence work. I had worked as the acting country director on many occasions and had access to security materials to some extent through the embassy.

Looking back, I understand where he was coming from. He was upset that I didn't agree to ET Dick. Some volunteers do try to bend the rules, but I didn't want to punish someone without a valid reason. My main responsibility was to support the volunteers and also to make sure that they were abiding by the rules and regulations according to the Peace Corps manual. In the past I had taken harsh action on those four volunteers who had used drugs.

Three months passed. The director told me that I needed to keep working on my language but that the probation was over. His attitude toward me changed a little, but even then, it was not easy to work under him. Finding a new job in Nepal would be hard, and I had been enjoying my job except for this incident. It was the most difficult eighteen months in my working history.

This director did similar things with other senior staff of Peace Corps / Nepal. The deputy director was also put on probation for three months immediately after the incident with me. He had thought he had a good relationship with the director, but he got into the same ditch. I don't even remember why he was put on probation. He was as unhappy as I was at that time.

Time passed slowly. The director eventually finished his two-and-a-half-year tenure in Nepal. I don't know whether he did not ask for an extension, as other country directors would do, or if his request was denied, but I was happy to see him go. I'm glad I continued with Peace Corps.

A Water Buffalo for a Dowry

The country director had just arrived from her official trip to Washington, DC. She came to the office directly from the airport and spent several hours meeting volunteers and staff. She left me a message saying she would like to see me early the next day. I thought she might want to discuss some programmatic issues that Washington officials had raised during her visit.

When I went to see her that morning, her first question was "What is this story about your volunteer Jim marrying a beautiful village girl and getting a water buffalo as a dowry?" She took out a postcard from her portfolio bag and shoved the card toward me.

I saw that it was a postcard of a well-known Indian film star. In fact, she was very beautiful, with an oval face, big black eyes, a small mouth, and well-shaped eyebrows. Curly wisps of hair dangled over her ears. She was wearing a pretty red *saree* with a golden border and a sleeveless short blouse with her saree tied seductively at her slim waist just below her navel. A lock of curly hair hung down to her waist. She had acted in so many Indian films that every teenage girl and boy in Nepal recognized her face. I could not figure out what my country director was talking about.

She explained that one of the senators had called her in Washington to ask about the issue. Jim's father had called the senator and requested that he find out what was going on, as his son had not responded to his letters. The senator was insistent and wanted to find out about the issue as soon as possible. Our director had talked to the father, who told her that he had planned to send Jim to medical school, but instead here was this astounding postcard saying he was going to marry the girl in the picture. And with a water buffalo as his dowry— how ridiculous! Jim also told his father that he no longer wanted to go to medical school but planned to settle permanently in Nepal.

I had no clue what was going on. This would have seemed absurd even for a Nepali. I had just visited Jim a month ago, and he had not mentioned anything about it. He was posted in a remote village in the Far Western region, and communication was difficult, as there was no telephone in his village. Letters usually took about eight or ten days from Kathmandu.

I told my director that I would find out what was going on. The only way to communicate with Jim was by wireless. For that he had to come to the district center, which was about six hours' walk one way. I went to the wireless office in Tripureswor and sent a message to the district education officer asking him to arrange for Jim to be at the wireless office at 12:30 p.m. next day.

The next day I went to the wireless office and put the call through. This was the old system where you had to send the message by means of Morse code, and the operator had to translate that into speech. I waited for a while, and the operator told me that Jim was on the line. I tried to converse with him but had no luck understanding a single word. Both of us were shouting loudly, but the sounds made no sense. We tried for a while, hoping that the line would get better and we would be able to talk, but it did not improve. I had to give the microphone to the operator and requested that he transfer what I had to say through Morse code transmission.

We communicated for a while as the operator translated from his Morse code message. Jim was doing well. He did not have any problems; teaching was going well, the food situation had improved since the start of monsoon, had brought fresh green vegetables. The teachers were friendly, and he was enjoying his teaching.

Finally, I asked him about the girl in the postcard and the dowry of a water buffalo. The operator was also puzzled when he heard my question. There was silence on the other side of the line. The operator waited for a moment, but there was no response to our question. I was getting nervous. Was it real? Was he going to get married to a Nepali village girl? Had he made up his mind? I asked the operator to repeat my question.

Finally, his response came, saying, "I'm sorry; that was just a joke! Obviously, my father didn't understand that it was a joke."

Looking back, it was indeed a great prank to pull on his parents, and I am sure Jim's father was able to laugh about it after the dust had settled down. But at that time, he was frustrated that he could not contact his son and did not realize that Jim was just making a joke. The idea of having a water buffalo as his son's wedding gift was the strangest thing he could have heard. This incident created a good deal of chaos and confusion among Peace Corps staff.

The Tomba Culture

Tomba is part of life in much of the eastern hills, especially in Limbu, Rai, and Sherpa communities. *Jand* is homemade beer made by fermenting millet that is strained so the grains are left behind. By contrast, tomba is also fermented millet, but it is not strained. It is served in a big tomba pot made out of bamboo or wood with lovely decorations. People who can afford to, decorate the pot with silver or other precious metal.

Drinking tomba

The tomba pot is about eight inches high and four inches in diameter. It is filled with fermented millet, and hot boiling water is poured on it at the time of drinking. Most people who serve tomba put a few grains of *chamal* (uncooked rice) in the pot—I don't know why. A bamboo straw is used to drink it. The straw is about ten inches long and notched on one side, and a tiny piece of bamboo is attached so that the millet grains do not come in with the water while drinking. If the tomba is good, people refill the pot two to three times. After the third refill, the alcohol is too diluted.

Once when I was visiting volunteers in the Tehrathum and Taplejung Districts, I had to make a side trip to Morahang. The trail forked at Tinjure, which means three peaks. There was fresh snow on the mountain slopes, and it was freezing cold. It was unimaginable that some of the porters were walking barefoot on these snowy trails. I was shivering even though I was bundled up in my down jacket with many layers of clothes. The porters were each carrying more than seventy kilograms of supplies and walking barefoot in the cold, snowy morning.

The Tinjure area is well known for the variety of colors of the rhododendrons. The months of April, May, and June are prime time for rhododendrons, but it was just the beginning of February, too early to be able to see the flowers. The trail to Tinjure is also known for its breathtaking view of the snow-capped mountains dominated by Kanchenjunga and Mount Everest. The trail had snow in patches. The white snow in the background and on the rhododendron trees made a beautiful contrast with the colorful emerging buds.

I made it to Morahang around six in the evening. It was twilight, and visibility was decreasing as I approached the village. It was my first trip to Morahang, and I had to find the headmaster's house. I was making a side trip to check out the school as a possible post for the coming school year. I needed to meet with the headmaster to discuss the science teaching situation and their need and willingness to work with an American Peace Corps volunteer. They also needed to provide housing for the volunteer.

I had no problem finding the headmaster's house. Everybody in the village knew Mr. Parshuram Khapung, and a group of children was eager to lead me to his house. I had never met Mr. Khapung before. As soon as we got near his house, the kids ran ahead and informed him that a stranger was coming. He was waiting outside his house when I got there. I introduced myself and told him the purpose of my visit. He went inside the house, saying he would be back in five minutes. A woman, who I later found out was his wife, came out with a blanket and spread it on the pindhi and told me to rest.

In a few minutes, the headmaster came out with a boy carrying two tomba pots. Then he explained to me that it is the Limbu way of welcoming a guest to the house. As I was not used to drinking tomba, I felt uncomfortable. He had already had his third refill of water while I was working on my first. After I finished my second refill, he said that it was dinnertime, and we went inside the house to eat. I was tired and hungry after the long day's walk. After my dal bhat around 11:00 that morning, I had just had a few cups of tea and some biscuits. I was very happy to be invited for dinner.

The kitchen was clean, and there were *gundris* (straw mats) and *radhis* (hand-loomed woolen rugs) spread around the fireplace. His wife was preparing dinner. The fireplace was the stove, and it heated the room. While eating, I told him there was a possibility we could post an American Peace Corps volunteer in his school and that we needed to go to the school the next day and complete a post survey form. He was happy to hear he might have a volunteer in his school. After dinner he showed me my room. I lit a candle after opening my sleeping bag. Then after a few minutes, he walked into the room with two tomba pots. I told him that I was not ready for the next tomba, but he kept insisting that while staying in a Limbu house I had to respect the local Limbu culture. He also said tomba was their main drink and that it was served for almost every occasion, especially to welcome guests and show respect to them. I had no choice but to accept it but had only a few sips after my second water refill. After he finished his tomba, he bade me good night and left the room. I read my book by the candle-light for a while and slept.

I woke up around 6:00 a.m. After my morning wash, I was ready to go to the school, which he had said was about forty-five minutes from his house. I was expecting a cup of tea to start my day, but Par-shuram came in with two tombas again! I told him that it was too early for an alcoholic drink, but he would not budge and said that it would be an insult if I did not drink the first tomba in his house. I just took a sip from the pot and told him to save it for me until we came back from school. It was already 8:00 a.m. when we left for the school. He had summoned the science teacher, as I had told him that I would like to see the science lab to determine if I saw the school fit for posting a math/science volunteer. The three of us left for the school at around 8:15 a.m.

On our way to school, I noticed a small tea shop. We stopped there for tea. I did not know whether he was joking or serious when he asked me if I was ready for the next tomba. He said that the tea shop provided the best tomba in the area. Thankfully, I was successful in avoiding tomba there. We reached the school around 9:00 a.m., and we completed our work around 1:00 p.m. I had to complete a thirty-five-page post survey that asked for details of the school, including the science laboratory, counterpart teachers for the volunteer, and housing and food situation. I found that the headmaster was committed to the development of the school. Two National Development Service (NDS) volunteers were also serving in the area at that time. NDS service was compulsory for all graduating students from Tribhuvan University (the only university in Nepal at that time). I happened to meet with them on our way to school. I discussed the possibility of posting a volunteer at the school, and they thought it was a good idea. One of the NDS volunteers, Mr. Krishna Prasad Bhattarai, came to work for the Peace Corps after he completed his master's degree. Currently he is the vice president at HRDC, where I served as an executive member of the board of directors.

It was a fruitful trip, but what I remembered most vividly was my encounter with tomba. I don't remember how many times I was offered tomba and how many times I declined, but it seemed that everybody drank tomba at any time of the day. Tomba was a must in any kind of celebration in this culture, and men, women, and even children partook.

When in Rome, do as the Romans do—but keep yourself sane.

My Second Encounter with Tomba

My next encounter with tomba was in Jirikhimti. This time I was visiting Nick, a volunteer who had been assigned to the local high school to teach mathematics and science. Jirikhimti is in the Tehrathum District, on the way to the district headquarters at Myanglung Bazaar. That afternoon I went to school, observed some of Nick's classes, gave him feedback, and discussed his food, living, and teaching situation. I talked to the headmaster about the need to find substitutes for Nick's classes if he ever had to go to Kathmandu for medical issues. We also discussed how his Nepali counterpart could help him by coteaching.

After coming back from school, we met two other volunteers, one from Myanglung and another from Okhre. It was Friday afternoon, so they had come after finishing the day's classes. Nick took us to the nearby tea shop where he ate his meals. I wanted to have a cup of tea, but the volunteers wanted to celebrate the weekend, so we ordered tomba and *sukuti* (dried meat). It was already 9:00 p.m. when we ate dal bhat and went to sleep.

The next morning, I had planned to go to Okhre. Since the volunteer from Okhre was already in Jirikhimti, we decided to go to Myanglung that day and go to Okhre only on Monday. It was strange, but I did not remember paying for the food and drink the night before, but the tea shop lady told me I had already paid last night. Probably I had been tomba *lagyo*—under the influence of the tomba. I might have had two tomba that night, but I was surprised that it had such an effect. Or maybe the volunteers paid for it and wanted to tease me for being a tomba lagyo Peace Corps officer?

Decision-Making

High intensive language training (HILT) was going on full swing, with four hours of language classes in the mornings and a few hours of technical and cultural instruction in the afternoon. This phase was the most difficult part of the training, as it was focused mainly on language. Also, the trainees had to live with a family to get in-depth exposure to Nepali culture. On weekdays, trainees would eat two meals with the family and have only midday snacks and tea or coffee at the training sites. They followed the Nepali work schedule, working six days a week with only Saturdays off. They were totally free on Saturday and were on their own for food that day.

I made a number of visits to the training site during this time and got to know the volunteers fairly well. It was customary that when a program officer went to visit the training site, he or she would observe one or two sessions each of the language, cross culture, and technical training classes. My first language class observation was a disaster. Instead of a language teacher, a technical trainer was teaching Nepali, despite having no language-teaching experience. He was translating each word. He would say something in Nepali and then translate that into English. Our language trainers were taught not to speak any English in the language class.

The Peace Corps uses the audio-lingual method for teaching language. This method emphasizes repetition and drill work. A sentence or a question is introduced, and every participant is asked to repeat after the teacher. The instructor might ask a question like "What is your name?" to one of the students. The student answers the question, saying, "My name is…" The teacher asks all the participants the same question, and each participant inserts his or her name and repeats the answer.

This technical trainer did not have any clue about the Peace Corps language-teaching methodology and was going completely against our training norms and standards. I stayed in the class for about twenty minutes and left. I asked the language coordinator why the usual language trainer was absent. The trainer had said he was going to go to Kathmandu Friday evening and would be back at the site Saturday evening. Instead, the coordinator got a call on Saturday from the language trainer saying he was scheduled for an eye operation. The coordinator called his home later to find out more about the situation. The trainer's daughter picked up the phone, and she did not know anything about the operation but that her father had just left home to visit one of his friends. The language coordinator had reported that to the project director.

It was Sunday morning when I observed the class. The trainer arrived later that afternoon while I was talking to the project director. I left the room to let the project director discuss the matter with him. After an hour, the project director came and said that he had decided not to take any action but sent him to resume teaching and warned him not to miss class again. I was not happy with his decision. It was not only his absence from the site but also the lie about having an eye operation. The trainer probably thought that nobody would call his house, so he had not told his daughter the story about the surgery. I was afraid that this incident might set a precedent for other training staff to become lax in their duties.

Even after a long discussion, the project director did not want to change his decision. I suggested he reconsider. After about an hour, he told me he had changed his mind and took disciplinary action, giving the trainer extra work and also not paying him for the days he was absent. Peace Corps training ran according to strict regulations, and people looked at past precedents while seeking to settle a problem. I think we made the right decision in this case.

After the completion of the HILT and family stay phase of the training, the trainees were divided into several groups, each of whom went to a different village for practice teaching. A language teacher was assigned to each group. The technical coordinator, cross-cultural coordinator, and administrative assistant took turns visiting the different sites.

After the practice teaching, I had completed all the post surveys and was ready to assign posts to the trainees. The trainees then had five days to select their posts.

Another Incident: Be Tough When Necessary

I remember another time when I had to step in and change a situation by using my authority. Visiting volunteers was not an easy job. Sometimes we had to walk for several days. Once in a while, we were able to drive on a gravel road to or from the roadhead or take a small plane to a local airport and walk from there.

On this trip, we had to drive for several days and also walk for several days to visit volunteers in the Far-Western Region. I took a Peace Corps driver with me so I could leave the vehicle at a roadhead town while visiting a volunteer. I would then come back and drive a few hours to another roadhead to visit another volunteer. We would continue doing this until we finished visiting all the volunteers in that area.

To visit with the first volunteer, I had to walk four or five hours from the roadhead to the volunteer's village, so I was planning to start early in the morning. We were on a long trip. After a long day's drive, I wanted to start my trip very early the next day so that I would be able to reach the volunteer's village before dark. But my driver told me he was tired and wanted to leave later the next day. On hot summer days, there is usually rain in the evening, and I wanted to finish walking before the rain started.

My driver on this trip was a pensioner from the Nepali army who had worked for the Peace Corps for about ten years. I was young and new in my job in the Peace Corps. The driver did not pay any attention to my polite request to leave early the next day. I was upset. I asked him, "Do I have to plan my trip according to your whims? If you don't want to start early morning tomorrow, you can go back to Kathmandu. Give me the key, and I will drive myself. You can go home and rest. Think it over. If you are willing to continue with me, you should be ready by seven in the morning." I left him and went to sleep. I don't think he was expecting such a strong reaction from a new Peace Corps officer.

The next morning, he knocked on my door at five minutes to seven to get my backpack and load it in the jeep.

The Royal Massacre

I had just arrived back from the US. My bedside phone rang at 1:00 a.m. It was the morning of June 1, 2001. I picked up the phone unwillingly. I heard my older brother's voice on the other end.

"Did you hear the news? Is it true?" he asked.

I asked, "What news? What are you talking about? It is just one in the morning."

"There's been a royal massacre," he said. "The whole family of King Birendra has been wiped out."

I told him that I had not heard anything but that I would call as soon as I did.

My brother had many connections in Kathmandu, including high-ranking politicians and army and police officers. One of his friends must have called him to inform him of what had happened at the royal palace that night. I was puzzled, wondering who would dare to take such a dangerous step at the royal palace. I was afraid to call anybody. What if it was just a rumor? I started thinking about my contacts, including senior army officers Brigadier Thapa, Lieutenant Colonel Shrestha, General Rana, and high-ranking police officers. I also thought of friends in politics, but I did not want to call any one of them at that wee hour of the morning. I decided to wait for a few more hours.

When I was trying to fall back to sleep, the phone rang again. I looked at my watch. It was 3:00 a.m. It was my nephew, Senior Police Officer Pankaj Shrestha, saying "Uncle, if you are planning to go out of Kathmandu, cancel all your plans. All five members of King Birendra's family and many other royal family members were killed in a palace massacre last night. There might be a curfew for a few days." He knew that my job involved traveling outside Kathmandu.

I asked him a few questions, but he said he was not in a position to answer. Either he did not know, or the information was considered confidential.

The dead included King Birendra, Queen Aiswarya, Crown Prince Dipendra, Prince Nirajan, and Princess Shruti. All five were from King Birendra's family. Other royal family members who died in the massacre were Dhirendra, King Birendra's brother (who had renounced his title to marry a European woman); Princess Jayanti, King Birendra's cousin; Princess Shanti, King Birendra's sister; Princess Sharada, King Birendra's sister; and Kumar Khadga, Princess Sharada's husband. In total ten people died but nobody died from Prince Gyanendra's family.

Prince Dipendra was pronounced king while he was in a coma. But the rumor was that he was already dead when he was pronounced king, and Prince Gyanendra was announced to be the "caretaker," as Dipendra was in a coma. Rumor was that he was pronounced king just to gain sympathy from the people. Three days later, Dipendra was pronounced dead, and Gyanendra was made king. Gyanendra had become the next in line to the throne after Dipendra and Nirajan's deaths.

King Gyanendra appointed a three-man commission to find out the facts about the incident. These three were Supreme Court Chief Justice Keshav Prasad Upadhyaya, Speaker of the House Taranath Ranabhat, and Communist Party of Nepal United Marxist-Leninist (CPN UML) leader Madhav Kumar Nepal. Madhav Nepal himself had expressed his interest in being on the commission but dropped out later under some pretense. The investigation concluded that Crown Prince Dipendra carried out the massacre. Many people in Nepal and abroad still do not agree with this conclusion, saying that the investigation was not carried out properly.

The report says that Dipendra was drinking heavily that night and that King Birendra told him to leave the party. Prince Nirajan and Prince Paras (Gyanendra's son) took him to his room. About an hour later, he returned to the party with MP5K and M16 assault weapons.

First, he fired at his father at point-blank range, then his aunt, uncle, and others. Then he took the lives of his mother, brother, and sister. Nirajan and Aishwarya followed Dipendra and confronted him in the garden, where both of them were shot. After that Dipendra shot himself and died in the garden.

Rumors started flowing! We learned that Princess Komal (Gyanendra's wife) was hospitalized for a few weeks, then went to London for treatment. Some say this was only a pretense, that her injuries were not severe. Paras also suffered minor injuries. It seemed that Gyanendra's family had been spared.

One rumor from people who had close contact with the royal family is that Prince Dipendra was angry with his mother over whom he should marry. Dipendra was in love with Devayani Rana, daughter of Pashupati Shamsher Rana and wanted to marry her. But Queen Aishwarya was against this relationship because of the historic animosity between the royal family and the Pashupati Rana clan.

Some people in Nepal suspected that Gyanendra had plotted the whole sequence of events with his son Paras and that he absented himself from the party by going to Pokhara the day before so that people would not suspect him. There were rumors circulating around Kathamndu that Gyanendra had a plane ticket ready to leave Kathmandu if the plan failed. The night of the incident, he started back from Pokhara and is said to have waited for news at the Baireni military barracks, returning to Kathmandu only after he confirmed that the plan had succeeded.

Another story was that Dipendra was mortally wounded by a gunshot to his left temple, but he was known to be right-handed. As both guns that had been used were at least twice the size of a revolver, it would have been impossible for him to shoot the left side of his face. This also points a finger toward Gyanendra, given that he had planned a trip to Pokhara that week and that only his family survived out of all royal family members who were present. As he was the undisputable heir to the throne, he would have had a motive and could have been the mastermind.

One retired army officer was assigned as one of several ADCs (aide-de-camp) to the then crown prince Dipendra. Keeping anonymity because he feared his life was in danger, he said that Dipendra must have been killed first, and that somebody wearing a mask to look like Dipendra had carried out the incident. He could not verify this, as only royal family members were allowed in that gathering. He says this from knowing Dipendra well and working closely with him for many years. He also says that Dipendra was so close to his family, he could not imagine him doing anything this heinous to them under any circumstances. Khagendra Sangraula, in his book *Raktakunda*, says that the queen mother Ratna's personal maid, Shanta, observed two men wearing masks. One of them resembled Crown Prince Dipendra, and they were firing shots at the massacre. Shanta's husband, Trilochan, along with other employees of the royal family, was also killed in the massacre.

Another rumor was that the then prime minister Girija Prasad Koirala was not allowed to go to see the bodies of the royal family but was imprisoned in a room in the military hospital where the dead and wounded were taken after the massacre.

A few days after the incident, I received an email with plans that had been detailed before the event. These plans clearly stated the intended movements of Paras and some generals close to the palace. It stated the time and route that they would be taking to enter the palace that day, implying that the massacre had been planned for a long time. I had been instructed by the sender to delete the email immediately after I read it, which I did.

People slowly started to speak about the incident. Retired army general Vivek Shah, who was ADC to King Birendra for a long time, published a book, *Maile Dekheko Durbar* (*The Palace I Saw*). He explicitly mentions the controversial fact that the Maoist insurgents had been trained by the Indian army in India, which both the Indian government and the Maoist party have disputed. Even though he was very close to the royal family, he did not divulge much about the royal massacre. We don't know why he did not want to discuss it.

In this book, General Shah endorses the official findings of the Ranabhat Commission that Crown Prince Dipendra was behind the massacre. He had proposed a full-fledged investigation, but King Gyanendra did not want to go deeply into the details of the massacre.

Another rumor was that no forensic tests were conducted on any of the royalty killed in the incident. Postmortems of the dead were not carried out. The rumor is that Queen Mother Ratna did not want the bodies mutilated in any way. The then prime minister Girija Prasad Koirala supported her decision.

Nine-Eleven

Jharana said, "I am in constant contact with Archana. She just hitch-hiked a ride with someone. She should be home soon." The two sisters were living in Vienna, Virginia, at that time. After graduating from Falmouth Academy in Massachusetts, Jharana went to Randolph Macon Women's College in Lynchburg, Virginia. Randolph Macon was a women's college that had recently become a coed school. At that time she was working for Verizon.

Archana followed in her sister's footsteps and graduated from Falmouth Academy and then attended Bryn Mawr College. Located near Philadelphia, Bryn Mawr has about 1,300 undergraduate and 500 graduate students. It is one of the Seven Sister colleges that were originally established for women.

After completing her undergraduate degree, Archana started working. Then both of them obtained master's degrees from George Washington University, Jharana in information technology and Archana in statistics.

Archana's graduation from Bryn Mawr

After completing her undergraduate degree, Archana applied for jobs at many firms and was worried when she did not hear back for some time. Eventually she was offered jobs by most of these companies and now faced the dilemma of deciding where she wanted to work. She accepted a job with Ernst and Young (a prestigious accounting firm) after long discussions with her sister Jharana. She was new to the job and also to the Washington, DC, area when terrorists attacked the Twin Towers in New York and the Pentagon, which is located just outside Washington, DC, in Arlington, Virginia.

The Twin Towers of the World Trade Center complex were located in the downtown financial district in Manhattan, New York, and contained 13.4 million square feet of office space. About fifty thousand people worked in the towers, and about two hundred thousand visited the towers every working day.

On the morning of September 11, 2001, four commercial planes were hijacked by nineteen Al Qaeda hijackers. Two of the hijacked planes crashed into the World Trade Center, at 8:46 a.m. and 9:03 a.m. The first hit the northern tower and the second the southern tower. The third plane hit the Pentagon on the outskirts of Washington, DC, at 9:37 a.m. The fourth plane crashed in a meadow in Pennsylvania at 10:03 a.m. after the passengers on board fought with and incapacitated the hijackers. Their ultimate target was said to be either the Capitol Building or the White House. The Twin Towers were completely destroyed. A memorial has been built at "ground zero," where the Twin Towers were.

Archana was already at work when the planes hit the twin towers in New York and the Pentagon in Virginia. She described the situation at her office. "For about half an hour, we did not know what was going on in the world outside our office building. We were all busy doing our work. Then around 10:00 a.m., I noticed people running around like crazy; it was chaotic. Finally, around 11:00 a.m., there was an announcement giving us whatever details they knew about New York and the Pentagon. They announced that the office was closed for the day. Everybody was ordered to leave the building."

In Kathmandu, I was watching CNN news around 8:00 p.m. I just could not believe it when I first saw the Twin Towers ablaze. Then came the news about the Pentagon. The minute I saw the news of the Pentagon, I thought about Jharana and Archana. I shared the news with Kamala, but she was not as panicked as I was. She said that girls would call if they were facing any problems. But I just wanted to hear their voices and find out if they were doing all right. I dialed their home phone in Virginia and also their cell phones. After many unsuccessful calls, I finally got hold of Jharana. It was a relief just to hear her voice. She was already home, but Archana was still on her way.

At that time, Archana's only means of transportation to work and back was the metro. All public transportation in Washington, DC, had been shut down, including the metro. Archana had no other way but to walk home from DC, which was about twenty miles. There were a lot people on the road. People did not know what to do. Archana later told us that she was about to call Jharana to come to fetch her, but she was successful in getting a ride with a stranger. Jharana said Archana had just called her to explain her situation when a car stopped and asked her where she was going. Luckily the man was also going in the same direction and offered her a ride. Archana called Jharana every five or ten minutes from the car, telling her where she was and what she could see from there. At the same time, Jharana stayed connected with me, explaining Archana's situation. Archana finally got home around 3:00 p.m., and all of us relaxed. Jharana said Archana was in tears of relief when she walked into the house. Then I finally had a chance to talk with Archana. The two sisters have always gotten along well and are best friends as well as sisters.

Our girls have grown up.

So Long

September 30, 2001. The time had come to say so long. Everybody who meets must depart sooner or later. It was time to say goodbye to all my friends and colleagues in Peace Corps. It had been over thirty years since I had first walked into the Peace Corps premises in Kamaladi near *ghantaghar* in Kathmandu. I had started as a language trainer and moved through many other jobs. Those thirty years had gone as quickly as thirty days.

The Peace Corps for me was the most prestigious school I could ever have attended. Today was my graduation day. The Peace Corps takes the Nepali government retirement age of fifty-eight as the mandatory retirement age for Nepali permanent staff. In Peace Corps language, I "extended for two more months" after my retirement date, meaning that I kept working at the request of the director in order to finish ongoing program work.

I had a few years of conflict with one country director, but in retrospect that seems minor in comparison with the rest of my time in the Peace Corps. Even during the difficult years, I remember receiving full support from my American counterpart, the associate director in charge of the English teaching program. Friends in need are friends indeed. Her support was invaluable to me at that time. Without her compassion I would have felt much worse.

I often got into trouble when I spoke up after seeing decisions being made that were unfair to the Nepali support staff. I still feel strongly that whenever I raised my voice, I raised it for good causes and for fair deals. The country directors and the administrative officers come to Nepal for two and a half years, and many had no prior experience working in Nepal. So we Nepalese took it upon ourselves to inform the American staff of the realities of life in Nepal, the volunteers' challenges, and how to navigate the government offices.

My long tenure in the Peace Corps allowed me to work with volunteers of different generations. This experience has given me a chance to look at the differences among the Peace Corps volunteers. Some of the earlier volunteers would return their living allowances saying that they did not need that much money to live in a Nepali village. In later years there were some who always needed more money from the Peace Corps. I don't know what brought this change. It could be the attitudes of the individuals, or their living styles, or it could be the economic situation of America; it could be anything.

I also saw a few volunteers who thought they could do as they pleased because they were volunteers. "I'm not an employee but a volunteer, so why do I need to abide by Peace Corps rules and regulations? Those rules are only for Peace Corps staff." I came across only a few volunteers who had this kind of notion. Yes, they were volunteers, but they were there with a job to do. Volunteers were not only responsible from eight to five, but twenty-four hours a day, more than a "real" job back home.

On the other hand, there were volunteers who took their jobs seriously and added extra projects to their assigned duties, such as teaching about health, hygiene, and nutrition. Some even built libraries, school latrines, or science laboratories as secondary projects. Many volunteers said they got more than they gave.

The volunteers were there because there were needs. I always remembered the Peace Corps' three goals, one of which was to provide technical assistance to the country they served. The volunteer is successful if they have achieved both technical transfer and cultural exchange.

Peace Corps is a unique institution. I got to serve my country while working for the US government. I traveled through seventy-two of the seventy-five (now seventy-seven) districts of Nepal. I met and got to know almost all the DEOs and SMTs of Nepal. That was possible only because of the Peace Corps. I don't know how much impact my service had on the field of education in Nepal, but I personally had a fulfilling career. I am satisfied with what I have done. I achieved what I could achieve in those years.

My experiences with the Peace Corps—the travel, the job difficulties, dealing with people in different situations, and the volunteers' safety and security issues—were all challenging at times. But these challenges were what kept me on the job for so long. Even though I did the same job for a long time, the people I dealt with were different, and the situations were different as well.

I felt I had done my job well, and it was time for me to graduate from Peace Corps. I was ready to begin a new life, but I was not sure where I would end up. Since my retirement, I have already crossed paths with many of my old volunteers and colleagues. I hope the friendships that we harbored will remain for our whole life. These are friendships I could not have made anywhere outside the Peace Corps. I bade goodbye to all my friends in the Peace Corps. So long.

After Retirement

Stopped by a Policeman

Close to my retirement, the country director encouraged me to apply for a green card (a permanent resident visa for USA). Non-US citizens working for more than fifteen years for the US government were allowed to apply for a special immigration visa. I was a little hesitant, but both of our daughters and Kamala encouraged me to try life in the US. I applied.

A few months after I applied, the US consular officer called me to his office and handed me a large sealed envelope, saying it had documents for Kamala and me. He instructed me to hand it over to the immigration officer when we entered the US.

The immigration officer at the airport stamped our passports with US work permits and told us that our green cards would be sent in a few weeks. We stayed with our daughters in Vienna. We soon applied for Social Security. Within a few weeks, both Kamala and I received our green cards and Social Security cards.

Getting a job in the US was not that easy. A friend of ours introduced me to the director of the Hubert H. Humphrey Fellowship Program, a division of the Institute of International Education (IIE). The director had served as a Peace Corps volunteer in Africa. The Hubert Humphrey Program targeted young and midcareer-level professionals, bringing them to the US for a one-year, nondegree graduate-level program for leadership development. I worked there for a few months as a volunteer.

I then got a permanent job with the Council for International Exchange of Scholars (CIES), a division of IIE. CIES conducts international exchange programs for scholars and university administrators. My main responsibility was to support the director in placing scholars from third-world countries in US host institutions to further their academic careers. I was also responsible for managing their US visas as well as administrative and logistical issues. These scholars were assigned mainly to historically black colleges and universities (HBCUs) and other primarily minority institutions. HBCUs were established before 1964 with the intention of serving black communities. I enjoyed tremendously working with these scholars from third-world countries with their different cultures, languages, and ethnicities.

Weekends were the only time I had for myself. A morning walk was (and still is) a pleasant routine for me that I started after retiring from Peace Corps / Nepal. Dr. Madhu Ghimire installed this habit in me immediately after I retired. Knowing that I would not be walking all over the country when I retired, he suggested I take a walk for at least an hour every morning. I have continued this practice since then whenever time permits, wherever I am in Nepal or in the US.

I usually left for work around seven in the morning and returned home only around six in the evening. It was about an hour's commute by metro. I got off at McPherson Square and walked to the office at 1400 K Street while working at Hubert H. Humphrey Fellowship Program. CIES was a little farther, near Cleveland Park in Washington, DC, so I had to start from home a little earlier in the morning. When new scholars were arriving in the US, and when we had seminars or conferences, my work hours increased by several hours a day. The American work ethic of not leaving anything on the desk for tomorrow has taught me how to manage my time. My work experience with the Peace Corps in Nepal helped tremendously while settling into my new job.

Every weekend, I spent at least one and a half hours on my morning walk. There would often be others walking. If you didn't look at them, they ignored you, but if you did, they wished you good morning and said a few words. When I moved to San Diego, California, I realized that I seemed to meet more people on my morning walk there than in Virginia or New Jersey. "Good morning; how are you?" "Hi, how are you?" "What a lovely day" are some of the greetings. Also, in the San Diego area, I noticed that almost every morning walker had a dog with them.

It was a weekend in the summer of 2005. I left home around six for my morning walk. I stopped at the Vienna metro station and picked up a newspaper. Then I continued walking toward Nutley Street. I was lost in my own thoughts when I heard somebody calling me. I looked over and saw a police car on the other side of the street. The policeman said, "Sir, wait there a minute." I was surprised and annoyed that a policeman was interfering in my personal life. He made a U-turn at the next intersection. He stopped and asked me a few questions. Where was I going? Where did I live, and where did I work? And a few more questions like that. Finally, he asked me if I had my photo ID with me. I wanted to tell him that he was interfering in my personal life, but I was also a little nervous. I always carried my Virginia driver's license with me. I pulled it out from my wallet and gave it to him. He looked at my license and looked at my face and said, "I'm sorry to bother you, sir."

I was confused and just wanted to ask him, "Officer (in America, the police are addressed as officer), what is the matter? Why are you asking me all these questions? What are you looking for?" But I didn't.

He explained that a man had accosted a woman at the Vienna metro station around six in the morning and ran away with her purse. He ran in the direction I was going. They were looking for that man. He described that man as in his forties, weighing about 145 pounds, and about 5' 6" tall with tan skin. Most likely a Hispanic man in his forties. I had heard of a few incidents of this kind before, so I was not surprised. Everything matched my description except for age. I asked the policeman if I looked like a forty-year-old man. He apologized for the inconvenience and said he was just doing his duty. He told me that the chopper flying over us had given him a lead about someone walking on Nutley, which was where I was walking. I had heard at least two helicopters hovering above me, I had no idea they would lead to this experience.

I praise the active security system of the US. Employing helicopters and cars to look for a man who stole a woman's purse! I was impressed with the politeness of the policeman. I was glad I had my ID on me. If I had not had my ID, I do not know what he would have done with me.

The Accident

It was the month of February 2006. It had snowed all night. The road had been plowed to clear the snow on the streets, but on both sides of the road, there were huge piles of snow, like seeing the Nepali Himalaya from a distance. It was the weekend, so I had the day off, but Kamala had to go to work. Her work was not far from home, so she usually walked, but I had that day off and volunteered to drive her to work. There was still ice on the road, so I was driving very carefully, in slow motion. I was talking to Kamala and driving. When I turned right, I turned into the second lane instead of the first lane, as I had to make an immediate left turn at the next intersection. I was not paying attention to the traffic coming from the left. The minute I turned to look, I heard something crashing into the left side of my car.

I stopped right in the middle of the road and looked all around my car. It was intact with a small scrape, and I heard a dinging sound. A lady came out of the other car and said, "Sir, let's park by that restaurant, and we can talk."

Kamala got out and started walking to work, as she was just a few minutes away. I followed the lady. It was freezing cold. I was not dressed for the cold, as I was just going to drop Kamala at work and come straight home. We drove to the restaurant parking lot. The woman told me she was going to call the police. I was worried. I had no experience with accidents in the US, and I didn't know what I needed to do. I called my daughter Jharana and explained what had happened.

The policeman arrived in ten minutes. He gave each of us a form and asked us to fill it out. The form required that I identify myself, the make and model of my car, and all insurance information. Luckily, I had all the papers in the car. It was bone-chilling cold. The policeman saw me shivering and came up to me and said, "Sir, why don't you fill out the form inside your car? It's cold out here." Then only I realized how cold it was.

We soon completed the forms. The police looked at our forms and asked us to exchange forms and get in touch with our insurance companies. That was all he said. I could not believe the issue was handled so easily.

Jharana and Bob (Jharana's boyfriend; they were not yet married) arrived. I told them what had happened. We went home and relaxed. We decided not to report the accident to the insurance company, as our car was not damaged. Reporting to the insurance company meant that premiums could be increased the next year. We were somewhat worried that the woman would report the accident to her insurance company. Most likely, she thought the same way we did, because her car was not damaged that badly either. The only thing I had noticed was that her front bumper was on the road. She had already picked up the bumper and had put it in the trunk of her car before we went to the restaurant parking lot.

This has been my only experience of an accident in US. When I saw my friend in Bangkok handling an accident, I thought this must be how the civilized world handles such things. No hassle and an easy solution to the problem. It would have been totally different in Nepal, with each party talking in loud voices with a crowd gathering around the scene.

My University Life

I completed high school in 1961 at Bhanu High School, Bandipur. After high school, I didn't have a chance to go to a formal college or university. I did all my higher education as a private student. Tribhuwan University (TU), the only university in the country at that time, gave this opportunity to all except science students. I was interested in medicine, but my financial situation did not allow me that option. I decided to study business, which was called commerce at TU. I completed my intermediate of commerce exam in 1966. I was working as a district cooperative manager and also teaching in the night high school in Chitawan at that time. I collected all the needed books and studied in my free time to prepare for my exam.

I took two months off from work and went to Kathmandu to prepare for and take the test. For those two months I studied very hard, probably sixteen to eighteen hours a day, including some private tuition classes. I still remember the difficulty I had preparing for one subject in my intermediate exam. I had no textbook for that subject. I went for my tuition (private class), and the professor lectured for about three hours and gave me the names of several books to buy and study for the exam. From the professor's house, I went straight to the bookshop and picked up the book I thought best and went home. I studied that book all night and took the exam the next day.

I completed my bachelor of commerce exam the same way in 1972. I had started working for the Peace Corps, and it was difficult to manage time for study. Most days I was working in training programs outside Kathmandu. There was no semester system, and the final examination was held once a year. English was my most difficult subject.

I completed my master of commerce exam in 1975. The annual exam had two parts, each of which had five papers. I was working in the General Services Office in the Peace Corps in those days. At the time of the second part of the exam, we had an auditor visiting from Washington, DC. I applied for a few days' leave to prepare for the exam, but the auditor told me, "I came here all the way from Washington to audit. How can the in-charge of the General Service Office be absent?" But he was good enough to allow me to take four hours off every day to take my exam. Every day as soon as I finished my exam, I rushed to the office. I was physically present at the office, but my mind was always thinking about the next day's exam. Even then, I was able to get a good score.

Except for some tutoring, I had no experience of college and university life until I joined Kathmandu University in 2008. In the Peace Corps, I spent most of my thirty years working in the education program. I had accumulated practical knowledge of how the education system worked in Nepal, but I had no theoretical knowledge. That void made me want to get a formal education. I had this goal while I was working, but my workload was too heavy. After retirement I did some work in Nepal as well as in Washington, DC, but my ambition to pursue higher education was still there. Before I retired, I had applied to several universities in the US and was accepted to the University of Massachusetts at Amherst and Teachers College, Columbia University (TCCU), but for various reasons was unable to join.

In 2006 I made up my mind and gave up my job in Washington, DC. I started looking for universities again. I decided to study in Nepal and went to see Dr. Kedar Prasad Shrestha, dean of the School of Education at Kathmandu University. I knew him from my Peace Corps days. At first, he did not believe that I was serious, maybe because of my age or my work experience. I was sixty-five years old at that time.

The following year I went again and met with the dean of education. Dr. Shrestha had retired, and Dr. Mana Prasad Wagley had become the new dean. After some discussion, he told me to apply for the MPhil, not the PhD. He explained that Kathmandu University requires either two master's degrees or one master's degree with thesis to enroll for the PhD class, but I had neither of these. I enrolled in the MPhil. course.

There were two professors present in my enrollment interview, the dean himself and another professor. I knew the dean from before, but the other professor was new to me. As soon as he entered the interview room, he said, "I know you." It happened that we had met in Pokhara, where he was a math teacher in a boarding school and I was running a Peace Corps training program.

The dean asked me to say something about myself and why I was interested in studying at my age and specifically at Kathmandu University. I think I talked for about half an hour; then the other professor asked me a few more questions. Finally, the dean asked about my ability to express myself in English. But I had already demonstrated this by answering his previous questions, so he assured me that I would be accepted. He warned me that up to now I had been writing for myself and for official purposes, but for my study, I needed to learn to write academically.

On orientation day, one of the other professors, Dr. Shree Ram Lamichhane, asked me what I was doing there. When I told him I was a student, he thought I was joking. I knew him from my Peace Corps days. He had been vice chairman of the Higher Secondary Education Board, while I had been APCD in charge of education. We had met frequently in those days to discuss volunteer placement and their progress in their jobs. Almost all these professors were my colleagues from my Peace Corps days, which was a little odd for me. Time and again, a professor would walk into a class and address me as "Joshee Sir." The other students stared at me as if I were a creature from a different planet. Most students were in their twenties or thirties; only a few were in their forties. At one point, I had to request my professors not to address me as "Joshee Sir," but to address me simply with my first name like the other students.

One day I was talking with another student. I happened to tell him that I had graduated from high school in 1961. He looked at me incredulously and said that even his father was born after 1961. It was fun to work with these young people from different backgrounds. Most of them were school principals or schoolteachers, but some of them were bank officers, some were from the Ministry of Education, and a few of them were working for NGO/INGOs or other government offices. They wanted to show me respect due to my age, but when they saw me behaving like one of them, they enjoyed it. Teamwork was fun. It did not matter who was the team leader; we always worked in a cohesive way. I was always interested in finding out the other team members' perspectives. Time and again I had to remind the professors to accept me as one of their students not as the colleague I was before. One advantage to being the seniormost person in the class was that I could easily speak with the professors, all of whom were younger than me.

We had a new professor for research methodology. He told us that he had never taught this subject before. We also noticed that whenever a student asked him a question, he tried to get the other students to answer and never disagreed with answer. He would say, "This is the way, I think, but you could be right too."

One day I confronted him and asked why he never corrected the students. He said that they are mature people and can think for themselves. He didn't see any reason to disagree with them even though their answers were not correct. I didn't agree with his point of view.

At the end of the session, the professor handed out an evaluation of the classes to complete. The questionnaire asked for the name and number of each student. I objected, saying that the evaluation should be anonymous. If we wrote our names, he would know who said what. But he insisted on collecting names on the evaluation sheets. We had an argument in front of the other students, and I said I would not do the evaluation for him. He was furious, saying that I was trying to influence the others to not participate. I think I was the only one who did not complete his evaluation form. I had disagreed with how he ran the class, which was why I refused to put my name on the evaluation, thinking that might have long-term consequences. He was not happy. I had to pay dearly for my decision in the coming years.

Most of the professors at the School of Education of Kathmandu University were competent and knew their subjects well. I noticed some would stay late at night searching the internet for relevant news so they could share those findings with the students. They were authorities in their area and always kept themselves updated. We were lucky to have that kind of talent and diligence in our professors.

I had my own problems going to school at this age. There were a lot of assignments and required readings. Retention had become a problem for me. I would read a page of a book and try to summarize what I had read. Sometimes nothing came to mind. Then I had to re-read the whole page. Sometimes reading twice was not enough; I had to keep reading the same page several times. Memorizing had been easy for me in high school. We used to easily memorize essays and geometry theorems, but at this stage of my life it had become a problem. In our MPhil. and PhD examinations, professors required us to memorize and cite references with the page numbers of the books or journals we cited. For these exams, I tried to remember fifteen to twenty references for each subject. This practice made me feel like I was back in high school, but now, because of my age, I had difficulty memorizing names and numbers.

I thought I did well in both of my qualifying exam papers. I passed the educational leadership exam, but I had to do an assignment for research methodology. As an assignment, my professor (the same professor I did not do the evaluation for) asked me to write a seven-thousand-word article related to my field of research. I spent several weeks trying to find articles to support my writing but could not find much. I wrote the professor for help, but instead he changed the topic of my assignment. This topic changing went on for a while until my assignment was finally accepted, and I cleared the qualifying examination.

Quest for Knowledge: Does Age Matter?

August 18, 2008. It was the second day of the second semester. My friend Mana and I took the bus that day, as I had left my car at the garage for a checkup. After the 8:30 p.m. class, we walked to Ring Road to catch a bus. It was dark. It looked like it was going to rain at any moment. We waited for the bus for fifteen or twenty minutes, but the bus did not come. We were going to flag down a cab, but finally a bus approached. We hopped in the bus.

The conductor came and asked for the fare. Before I took out my wallet, Mana gave the boy a twenty-rupee bill. The conductor said the regular fare was twelve rupees per person. Mana told him that we had student identification cards. The conductor wanted to see them. I hesitantly handed him my student ID card. It was the first and only time I used my ID to get a student concession for a bus ride. Mana also gave his card to him.

The bus conductor looked a little confused. He repeatedly looked at my card and at my face. As both of us were studying in the same class, we had identical cards except for our photos. The bus conductor threw a question at us. "Do you both study in the same class?"

I could see where the question was coming from. I was sixty-five years old, whereas Mana was just twenty-eight.

Mana said, "Yes. Both of us study in the same class."

The bus conductor couldn't believe that a man of my age was going to school with someone who could easily be my grandson. He kept our cards until we got to Koteswor. Near Koteswor he muttered, "How can this old man with gray hair be going to school with this young man? It is a scheme to save a few rupees. I know you can get a fake card for fifty rupees."

Mana got upset and told the conductor that he would pay him

one thousand rupees if he could get a fake ID card from Kathmandu University. The conductor silently gave us our cards back.

Two teenage girls also got off the bus at Koteswor. They suggested that I should dye my hair if I wanted to use my student ID card in the future. So other passengers also thought I was using a fake card. Or maybe the girls believed me but suggested I dye my hair just to make it easier.

After I got home, I thought about what had just happened. Why didn't that bus conductor think I was a real student? He might have seen others with fake ID cards in his bus. How did they make fake ID cards? Did people really do that just to save a few rupees on a bus ride? Why did people go through the hassle of making a fake ID card? Were we Nepalese so dishonest that we would make fake ID cards?

There were also other questions that hit me. Why did he not trust me? Was I too old to go to school? Why did the girls suggest I dye my hair? Did we have an age bar on going to school? When should people stop thinking about their higher education? Did Nepalese not have a concept of lifelong learning? Knowledge is power. Learning should be a self-motivated pursuit of knowledge. Learning is a key to personal development. For me, attending a university was something that I did not get to do when I was young.

There were 865,000 college students over the age of thirty-five in 2006 in the United States.[1] Adult education in Nepal tended to include only basic literacy and numeracy. I didn't know where I would apply the knowledge I was gaining; but I was just interested in acquiring knowledge.

My friends also asked me what I would be doing with my degree. I was not going to school to make my resume look attractive. So why was I a full-time student? Are you going to school to get a certificate to

---

1 U.S. Census Bureau, 2006

hang on your wall?

By then, both of my daughters had finished graduate school and were settled in their jobs. I was retired but not ready to just stay home. Maybe it was the "empty nest" syndrome that lured me to go back to school? I had free time on my hands, and I wanted to utilize it to gain some knowledge.

I didn't know how I was going to use my MPhil. and PhD degrees. There was no practical justification for studying. I just wanted to acquire more knowledge. I had already had a successful career. I didn't consider it a bad idea to obtain a degree with no plan or goal for its utilization in the future. That said, I would not mind putting my higher education to use to help develop the education system of Nepal.

I was thrilled to be able to actually attend classes at a university. As a coincidence, my MPhil class started in the same month when my younger daughter enrolled in the Wharton School of Business at the University of Pennsylvania. She resigned from her job as a manager at Ernst and Young, one of the five biggest auditing companies in the US, to return for her master's degree. My elder brother had completed his masters in political science when he was sixty-eight years old. I was seventy-four when I completed my PhD. Maybe it is in our family's genes to quest for higher education at an older age?

Experiencing Academic Hegemony

When I enrolled for my MPhil. program at the age of sixty-five, I got so many questions and so much advice from professors and from academically oriented friends:

"Why do you want to study here in Nepal instead of studying in America?"

"What would you like to do after you get your PhD degree? Will you be looking for a teaching job?"

"Never say no to your thesis supervisor even if you don't agree with him/her. If you have to say no, wait for an appropriate time, circumnavigate the situation, and bring it up politely."

"You will have to alter your professional writing to do academic writing. Academic writing is based on references in your area of study."

The first semester went well. My professional writing teacher thought I might not need to attend his class because of my long experience in professional writing, such as proposals and reports at different stages of projects. But I was back in school to learn whatever I could learn, so I did not want to miss any classes.

It was a new learning experience in many ways, both positive and negative. We had some disagreements with some of our professors, especially with one who wanted to teach us in the *gurukul* fashion (referring to the old practice of students staying at the guru's residence and learning by memorizing). There are some benefits of rote memorization, but I don't think that it is the most effective way of learning. It is helpful to memorize mathematical tables and mathematical and scientific formulas, but not page numbers and other details of references we were required to quote in our exams.

All my life I had been advocating for student-centered learning, which is constructive and long lasting because it is based on students' needs and understanding rather than memorizing what the teacher considers important. It allows students to be fully engaged in the learning process. It was surprising to see rote memorization being used by a professor in the School of Education, where I expected they would be trying out the latest teaching methods. Otherwise, how were we to meet the needs of our technologically advanced world? Take-home exams and writing papers at home could have easily replaced the three-hour classroom exam. This would have allowed us to use reference materials and cite them appropriately in our papers.

Learning theories describe how students learn, giving central focus to processing, absorbing, and retaining knowledge. There are different learning theories, but we should be able to select the one that best fits our environment and best helps us reach our goals.

Once one of my classmates and I were not happy with the grades we got from one professor. We asked him why we received only Cs instead of B+s or As, as we had expected. We were surprised to hear him say, "You are established in your profession. You are not going to use your grades to advance your career. So why do you need a high grade?" We thought it was a very unprofessional response.

In my PhD program, I had two thesis supervisors. One supervisor closely guided my work, whereas one time the other supervisor returned a ten-page paper to me after three weeks, saying he did not have time to read it.

Unfortunately, my original thesis supervisor's contract ended at the end of the year, and the university did not renew it due to some problem in their working relationship. I was left with my second supervisor, who by that time had not actually read my thesis. He sat in my departmental viva voce (an oral examination for academic qualification) examination, and he also sat on my preliminary viva presentation. He had few comments or suggestions in those presentations. However, after my final thesis presentation, it seemed he started reading parts of each chapter and then insisted I revise the entire thesis. As my other supervisor had already left, I had no choice but to work with him. I had wanted the views and ideas of the research participants to stand as my findings, but the thesis supervisor wanted me to present his ideas instead. My aim had been to leave all my mental baggage at home during my research interviews so the interviewees' ideas would be the findings. But he wanted his ideas to be my findings.

My thesis had already been reviewed by three external reviewers—two American professors and one Nepali professor. Their reviews were positive except for some minor comments. As my supervisor kept refusing to call a meeting of the thesis committee, I was worried about not being able to complete my degree even in my fifth year, one year after my final defense. My friends and other professors were also worried for me, but they could not do anything.

One day I gathered my courage and asked the supervisor to either give me a reason for not accepting my thesis or to approve it. Only then did he call a meeting of the thesis committee. He told me that the thesis committee members might ask me to present my paper again. He also told me that I should be ready with my matrix (a chart including the main comments from the reviewers and the changes I had made in my thesis based on their comments) on the scheduled date. Since I had already made my final presentation, the research committee members said I did not need to do the presentation again. They gave me some minor suggestions, and the committee unanimously approved my thesis.

Academic hegemony happens in most academic institutions, to a greater or lesser extent. My view is that the focus should be on finding a path to help students in their research work rather than harassing them. Students should be guided from the beginning about the proper way of writing a thesis and should not be pushed to include ideas that were not their findings.

The Presentation

It was the end of June. I was busy preparing for a team presentation at the university and also packing to leave for a trip to the US. When I checked my voice mail that Friday evening, there was a message from Gulf Air saying that there was a problem with my reservation and to come to the Gulf Air office today or early Sunday. I could not figure out what the problem could be. It was already 7:00 p.m., so I had to wait until Sunday morning.

Our MPhil team presentation was scheduled for Sunday afternoon. Saturday morning after breakfast, I went to the university to work on a "tracer" study, looking at students' employment after graduation and to what extent their field of study was used in their job. As we had discussed the day before, Tara Sir, one of my teammates, was supposed to be at the university, but he called and said that he was in line for gas, and it could take another hour. I started working on chapter four of our research, interpreting data that we had collected from the former MPhil and PhD students of the Kathmandu University School of Education. I had finished interpreting chapter four when Tara Sir arrived, and both of us started working on chapter five. I was thematizing the suggestions from research participants. Tara Sir was working on the methodological framework of the study. Sunday was our preliminary presentation day. But we were far from completing our writeup. We departed around 6:00 p.m. to meet again on Sunday morning.

On Sunday morning, I went to the Gulf Air office only to find that there were two bookings in our name. They could have left that message in the voice mail, and I could easily have informed them to cancel one of the flights. After resolving the issue with Gulf Air, I returned to the university. All four members of the research team, Toya Khanal, Basu Subedi, Tara Poudel, and I started working. We completed our PowerPoint and prepared for the presentation. All four of us were PhD students. The university had awarded us the contract to do this study.

We were tired and left for tea without even looking at our watches. While on our tea break, we got a message that the professors were waiting for us. We gulped down the tea and ran to the presentation room. We felt ashamed that we had made the faculty wait for us. Toya Khanal introduced the study and discussed how we had recruited the research participants. He explained the difficulties we faced trying to get some of the former students to complete the questionnaire. Basu Subedi then explained how we had processed the data and our methodological framework. I then presented how we had interpreted the data and what the data showed, how the university impacted the students' lives, the percentage who liked the way it was, and the percentage who wanted to see it changed. Then Tara Poudel explained the findings and made the concluding remarks. Even though we had started late, it went well.

The professors gave their comments, most of which were positive suggestions for the final report re: methodology and writing style. I felt lucky to be part of this great team. Despite our age differences, we became good friends and supported each other throughout our MPhil and PhD journey.

The Squeaky Wheel Gets the Grease

It was the day for our departure for the US. Kamala and I left home around 5:00 p.m. Check-in at Tribhuwan International Airport was easy. A young man with a smiling face looked at our e-tickets and US permanent residency cards (green cards) and said he was able to bump us up to business class. We happily collected our e-tickets, green cards, and luggage tags and took the escalator to the gate. After some time, we were called for boarding.

After a few hours' layover in Bahrain, we boarded the plane for Frankfurt with no problem. The problems started in Frankfurt. We landed at terminal two, and our flight was to take off from terminal one, gate one. We didn't have boarding cards, so we went back to the gate where we had landed to inquire about our flight. Then we went back to the gate one counter, but the person at the counter told me to wait. After fifteen or twenty minutes, we approached him again, but he told us to wait again. We were confused and didn't know what was going on.

After checking all the passengers, he called me and said that our reservation had been canceled. There were no seats either on an upcoming or the next flight, so we had to wait until the next day.

I was very upset. I told him I hadn't canceled our reservation, that we had come all the way from Kathmandu and that no one had told us that our reservation had been canceled. I told him we would be going on that flight and that he would need to call the police to remove us and that he would find the incident in tomorrow's newspaper. He told me to talk to the reservations department, as they handled reservations. I responded that I didn't know about any departments, that we just needed to continue on our flight because our reservations had been confirmed.

Only then did he called his supervisor, and he told her the problem. The supervisor approached me politely and told me that she would do whatever she could to help. I knew there was another United Airlines flight to Dulles airport one hour after ours. I said I would agree to go on the next flight if she would cooperate with me. I told her that my daughter would panic if we did not arrive on our confirmed flight and that she needed to arrange a telephone call so we could talk to our daughter. She agreed to that. I told her that we would take the next flight only if she could bump me either to first class or business class. If not, I would not give up my seat. She explained that the next flight was totally full and there was no way she could arrange to put us on that flight.

I said, "If you can cancel our reservation, why can't you cancel someone else's reservation to accommodate us?"

She eventually started phoning people.

Our flight was already closed by that time, so she worked to get us on the next flight. She asked us to wait awhile and returned saying she had two seats for us on the next flight in business class. She asked me for our daughter's phone number; she dialed the number herself and let me talk to our daughter. Everything worked out, and we flew in business class from Frankfurt to Dulles.

I had just learned that talking to customer service representatives is an art of negotiation. It never hurts to ask what they are able to provide in order to compensate you for the inconveniences they have caused.

The Departure

Once my mother and I were discussing a financial matter. When we could not reach a decision, my mother told me, "Ambika, ask your *atmaa* (soul) and act accordingly. *Atmaa* never lies." She would say that my *atmaa* would never lead me down the wrong path. It's only greediness and selfishness that leads down the wrong path. Probably because of this philosophy, she became a member of Brahmakumari Rajyog, a Hindu spiritual movement that proclaims that all human beings are the sons and daughters of Lord Shiva and that all are equal—there are no higher or lower castes. It also teaches the theory of "Live and let live."

Brahmakumari involves a form of meditation that relaxes the mind and nurtures a healthy balance between our inner and outer worlds. The instruction from your *atmaa* is pure, unselfish, and selfless, and it can guide you in the right direction if you listen to it carefully. Brahmakumari preaches respect for all faiths. Following Brahmakumari meant that my mother was a pure vegetarian. She renounced eating even onions and garlic. Even though she did not eat meat, she never showed hatred against those who did.

I was in Chitawan for three days visiting my mother. I had not seen her for a whole year, as I was in the US that year and had just come to Nepal a few weeks before. I quit my job with IIE (Institute of International Education) and Lion Bridge, a firm that provided interpreters for courts and hospitals where I worked as a Nepali language interpreter. After resigning from my last job with Lion Bridge, I had plenty of time to spend with friends and relatives in Nepal on this trip. After spending three days with my family in Chitawan, I had left for Kathmandu.

I got a phone call from my sister Bidhya in a few days saying that our mother wanted me to return to see her again. As I had told her that

I had a busy schedule in Kathmandu, I could not figure why she was summoning me back to Narayangarh.

I called my younger brother, Murari, and asked him if he wanted to join me. We left early the next morning. I called Bidhya before I left home, and she said everything was all right. Then we got to Mugling and called again. This time Bidhya was not available, so we talked to her husband, Ramhari *jwain* (brother-in-law). He told us that our mother had been rushed to the hospital a few hours before and that our sisters and older brother were at the hospital. We figured we would find out what had happened after we got to Chitawan.

We arrived in Narayangarh around 2:00 p.m. and found out that my mother had passed away around noon and that her body had already been taken to Devghat for cremation. They were waiting for our arrival, so we went directly to Devghat. We had a lot of discussion about the death rituals. My elder brother, who was a staunch communist, a believer in Marxism and Leninism, and a follower of Mao, thought the usual Hindu death rituals were based in superstition, and didn't want to go through those rituals. Usually the sons of the deceased shave their heads, live separately in a secluded place for thirteen days, and cook their own meals. But after much discussion, we were able to persuade him to participate for the sake of the local people and our family members, especially the more traditional female members of the family. Social and religious rituals still play a big role in our culture. Such practices are difficult to give up even if we do not believe in them. We were glad we were able to persuade my older brother to comply.

I was curious to learn how our mother had died within such a short period of time. We heard she was fine at 10:00 a.m., when we called my sister Bidhya from Thankot, but we then found she died at noon. Bidhya, my nephew Gaurav's wife, told me that she was with *aji* (grandma) until the last minute. She combed her hair and was talking to her. Then *aji* said she wanted to rest a while. Bidhya left her lying down on her bed. After half an hour, Bidhya heard her breathing heavily. She saw something was wrong and called my elder brother. They rushed her to the hospital. The doctors immediately pronounced her dead.

I heard from our family members that she had been doing all her household tasks by herself till that day. At ninety-six she was still active with no sign of weakness or illness until she bade farewell to this world. She took a bath that morning without any help. She ate her regular meal, then went to take an afternoon nap.

She was lucky to have such an easy death, without giving any trouble to anybody. Maybe her *atmaa* told her she did not have many days to live, so she wanted to see me for the last time. It was my great misfortune that I could not fulfill her last wish. I just hope that I will also have as peaceful a death as she did. Her departure was sad, but it is said that we meet only to part and that we are born only to die. We will also have to follow this same path one day.

After thirteen days of mourning, we came out of seclusion and finished our rituals. Then my elder brother, Madan Mohan Joshi, and I deposited some money in a bank to start a scholarship program in her name. We both agreed that that would be what our mother would have wished. This program provides scholarships to two promising but underprivileged students in the eleventh and twelfth grades every year. Later, we shared our idea with all our mother's siblings, and all of them contributed to help fulfill her dream of making education attainable to those who otherwise would not be able to attend. This scholarship was established for the students of Narayani High School, which I had helped to start.

We also started a scholarship program at Bandipur Campus in her name, focused mainly on students of poor and low-caste families studying in eleventh and twelfth grades, who would not be able to continue their education without this scholarship. Through these small scholarship programs, we hope to keep our mother's love for education alive. I bid farewell to my mother, the guru of my life.

Religion

My mother followed the teachings of Brahmakumari Rajyog in the latter part of her life. She practiced wholeheartedly as a Brahma Kumari. This made her happy, and I was happy that she was happy. I personally do not follow any religious sect. My mother and Kamala would often ask me to take them to the temple. I would happily comply, but I do not believe in worshipping or offering flowers and money to these idols. So I would accompany them to the temple gate and return to the parking lot and read a book. I mentioned that our wedding ceremony was held at Budhanilkantha temple. I agreed to this in order not to make anyone upset. Similarly, if my mother or Kamala asked me to perform a certain *puja*, I would go along to make them happy. If they were happy, the whole family would be happy and the home peaceful.

Talking about religious beliefs reminds me of our thirteen-day mourning rituals after the demise of my mother. On the second day, there was a big discussion about the custom of having a priest recite and explain the verses of the Garud Puran at our house for five or six days. The Garud Puran belongs to Vaishnavism (the Hindu denomination centered on Lord Vishnu) and consists of Lord Vishnu's explanation of the meaning of human life to his vehicle Garuda, the king of the birds.

The female members of our family and also the neighbors wanted to have the Garud Puran, but we three brothers did not. Much of the Garuda Puran warns about the suffering of the hell realm. Yamraj, the king of death, punishes those who sinned during their lives. My brothers and I especially did not like the way the priests usually explain the Puran to benefit themselves. They will say that the deceased person is on the way to his or her heavenly abode but needs certain things to complete the journey. These things can be a good milk cow or warm clothes or whatever the priest wants—the priest himself receives all the items that are offered.

A Nepali anecdote illustrates this. The priest demands good clothes, a good bed, a cow, shoes, and so on, saying that the deceased person needs these things to live comfortably. One family comes up with an idea. On the tenth day of the ritual, the priest asks the oldest son to give certain expensive things. The son tells the priest that he had a dream in which his father was suffering from very bad knee pain and that his father told him to heat a metal spatula until it is red hot, then put it on the priest's knee, to cure the father's pain. The priest understands and changes to saying that that the family can offer whatever they like, that it is not necessary to provide everything that the Puran says.

This is where we had our disagreement with the female members of our family. Finally, we compromised on a solution. We were able to convince everybody that several days of Brahmakumari lectures given by one of the sisters of Brahmakumari would be the right way of paying tribute to our mother. This worked out perfectly as we followed our own mother's chosen path.

There are various other issues related to these rituals. In Newari culture, the daughters cook seven *manaa* (about fifteen pounds) of rice along with vegetables and *daal* on the seventh day after the death. This is called *Nhehnumaa Beu* (*Nhehnumaa* means "on the seventh day," and *Beu* means "to give"). Traditionally, these foods were taken away by *Chyaame* (the "untouchable" *Newari* sweeper caste), but now the Chyaame reject this food, and it is fed to cows. Newars are *vaishyas* (traders or business people) with their own subcaste system divided according to hereditary occupations. These are some examples:

Byanjankaar: Chefs
Chitrakaar: Artists
Halawaai: Sweet-makers
Madhikarmi: Bakers
Mali: Gardeners

Rajabhandaari: Storekeepers

Vaidhya: Aayurvedic doctors

Raja Vaidhya: Royal Aayurvedic doctors

There are huge paradoxes within the caste system in Hinduism. Among the Hindus there are *Shudras* (untouchables), *Vaishyas* (business people such as Newars), *Kshatrias* (warriors and rulers—Kshatrias and Thakuris), and Brahmins (priests, the highest caste of the Hindus). Caste discrimination is not going to be eliminated easily. I am most worried about the way the Dalits or Shudras, the low-caste people, are treated, which affects their social and financial situation and their access to education. A strict law and its harsh enforcement may be needed to provide some relief to these people.

In Hinduism, to me the most abhorrent aspect is the caste system. Even though it is not a part of the religion, it is so intertwined with Hinduism that it is seen as part of it. I am not an idol worshipper. I do not do any kind of prayer or *puja*, and I have a hard time believing in reincarnation. But I am not a nihilist. People need to have a goal to achieve meaning in their life. To me, a meaningful life is doing no harm to others but helping needy people, and living a happy life without anxiety or jealousy. I accept the parts that I like from different religions.

सर्वे भवन्तु सुखिनः, सर्वे सन्तु निरामयाः ।
सर्वे भद्राणि पश्यन्तु, मा कश्चित् दुःख भाग्भवेत् ॥

May all beings be at peace, may no one suffer from illness,
May all see only auspiciousness, may no one suffer.

Among different religions, Buddha's teaching attracts me the most. The truth that comes from your inner soul should be your law. Nirvana is the goal of Buddhism. But I have a hard time believing in reincarnation, whereas many Tibetan Buddhists do. For example, as soon as the

Dalai Lama and other reincarnate lamas die, the followers go searching for the newborn lama. They do test the baby to see if he can identify objects from his past life. If he passes the test, he reclaims the status of the former lama. I have a hard time believing this.

Jesus preaches "God is love." God is omnipotent. Love everyone. Love is the heart and soul of human beings. Islam believes in one god, Allah. There is only one god. All of these religions talk about Nirvana, Salvation, and Mokshya, none of which influences me that much. I accept the parts that I like from each religion. I would rather be fully aware of my surroundings and try to help a needy person, or the environment, or whatever presents itself.

In the Gita, Lord Krishna says, "Sarva-Dharman parityajya mam ekam sharanam vraja सर्व धर्मन् परित्यज्य मम् एकम् शरनम् व्रज." Abandon all other religions and come to me. You will get salvation. You will get Nirvana. I have great difficulty accepting this. He seems to say that his religion is the best. Everybody thinks theirs is the best.

Charvak goes to the other extreme, saying to enjoy your life as much as you can. Don't worry about tomorrow. Who knows what will happen tomorrow? Your cremated body is not going to come back again. He says:

yada Jeevam, Sukham Jivet, Rinam Krityam, ghritam pibet
bhasmi bhutasya dehasya, punaragamana kutah?

यद जिवम् सुखम् जिवेत् रिनम् क्रित्यम् घ्रितम् पिबेत्
भस्मि भुतस्य देहस्य पुनरागमन कुत?

As long as you live, live happily. Borrow money and drink ghee. The body that has been burned will not come back.

I'm not Charvak's follower either. I look at the world from a different angle. Working for the betterment of human beings is the best spiritual work for me. Helping the poor and providing food for the hungry is the utmost in religious work. Keep people happy. Jealousness and rivalry should not have any place in this world. Vasudhaiva Kutumbakam (वसुधैव कुटुम्बकम), a phrase from the Upanishads, provides a broad spectrum of human life. *Vasudha* means earth, and *kutumbakam* means family. The whole world is one family. This phrase emanates the interconnectedness of all lives. *Gaansa, Baasa,* and *Kapaasa* (गान्स बास र कपास food, shelter, and clothing) are basic human rights. Therefore, everybody in this planet should have access to these basic needs. People should make a living wage and not have to work two full-time jobs to meet their expenses. This philosophy tries to foster an understanding that all living beings of this world are one family.

Observation

When you walk into a different culture and a different surrounding, there is much to learn and observe. My trips to the US have given me many such occasions. On my first trip, I was surprised to see that there were trees and well-maintained landscaping in public places all over the country. The forests were so well preserved that I wondered how they met their need for forest products. Taking care of the surroundings and preserving nature seems well worth the money spent on it. Even though US residents have to pay high taxes, the tax payers' dollars are utilized for the benefit of the people and the society.

Roads are fixed in a timely fashion if there are problems. Trees and landscaping in parks and public places are well maintained. People see the proper use of their tax dollars, and they do not hesitate to pay a little higher state and federal tax.

Historical places are preserved equally well. On my first visit to America, I visited colonial Williamsburg in West Virginia, a living history museum, which was founded in 1699. I was amazed to see how well they have tried to teach history to the new generations through recreating the past. I remember seeing a presentation of how gunpowder was made. The people working there wore costumes like the people of those days. Even the speech was archaic. What a wonderful way to learn about history!

Our trip to Mount Vernon was another lesson of history. We were amazed to see how they have preserved the estate of the first president, the historic home of George and Martha Washington. Again, it is a living museum where we visited the tombs and the slave memorial, and we talked to people dressed as George and Martha Washington.

Even though things may look ordinary to the residents of this country, for people who are visiting, especially those from a third-world country, the upkeep of the surroundings, people's behavior, and many more things are impressive. Just simple and ordinary things give plenty of food for thought. The above are just a few examples of the many things I noticed, and the following are some more of my observations.

Drinking from the Tap and Waterborne Diseases

You can drink water straight from the tap. Yes, you can drink water without filtering, boiling, or treating it. This is hard for people from developing countries to believe. In Nepal, after Peace Corps trainees arrive in the country, the medical office provides a series of lectures for staying healthy in Nepal. The first is on how to avoid waterborne diseases.

Waterborne diseases are caused by microorganisms in water, un-peeled fruits, and anything else we eat raw. Transmission may happen while taking a bath, washing, or drinking. Careless preparation of food could also transmit these diseases. According to the World Health Organization, 3.4 million people die worldwide from waterborne diseases every year (Berman, 2009). The joy of being able to drink from the tap is indescribable. In Nepal, people either don't care and get sick frequently, or they do care and spend a lot of time and money assuring that their water and food are clean. Some of my relatives say that I taught them how to treat their water so that they do not get sick from waterborne diseases. They appreciate that and say that is the reason they are staying healthy.

Water scarcity is a problem in certain parts of America. Recycled water may be used for gardening with clear signs saying "In order to conserve water, reclaimed water in use. Do not drink." Parts of America use a drip irrigation system, which provides a limited amount of water, to preserve water. Southern California has a semidesert climate. In San Diego County, drought has wreaked havoc and increased the likelihood of wildfires. We could learn from the steps this county is taking. They encourage installing artificial lawns (synthetic turf) and planting drought-resistant shrubs. Desalination is one way the San Diego region has tried to meet their water needs. The Carlsbad desalination project is one of the largest in the world and the largest in the Western Hemisphere (Joshee 2015).

Pets

"My son is twenty years old now, and he went to college last year. My daughter just went to college this fall," she said. Most likely she was in her mid- or late forties. She continued. "Because I have an empty nest, I acquired these two dogs. They are like my children." She was walking a Dalmatian and a German shepherd. The Dalmatian was a puppy, but the German shepherd was a full-grown female. One afternoon while I was walking our dog, she explained about her dogs and how she had inherited them. It's a common phenomenon in the US to adopt dog(s) after the children leave home.

She told me that the Dalmatians' roots are traced back to Dalmatia in Croatia in central Europe (part of Yugoslavia before 1991). Dalmatians are loved for their unique black spots on white fur. I did not ask how old the Dalmatian was, but it probably weighed about eight kilograms, and it was about ten inches tall. It was a beautiful male puppy. The German shepherd was much larger. These dogs originated in Germany and are well-respected guarding and herding dogs. They are very loyal and very protective of their masters.

This is the type of conversation that would take place while walking a dog or taking a relaxing morning walk in a neighborhood. Dogs and cats are the most popular pets in the US. Dogs also provide companionship to elderly adults. People believe in the physical and emotional benefits of owning a pet. Visually impaired people also keep trained Seeing Eye dogs to guide them. Having a dog as a pet is like childless parents adopting a child. It can be quite expensive. We have animal hospitals in Nepal, but in the United States it is not unusual to find dog hotels and places that groom dogs.

If you are busy or if you are going to be out of town and can't take your dog with you, people will take care of the dog for some amount of money. Either this person will take the dog to his/her own house or come to your house, feed them, and take them out several times a day. Or one can pay to leave the dog at a pet hotel.

People in the US are also very careful about sanitation. We see signs on trails and in parks saying "Clean up after your dog." In parks, the local government provides plastic bags near the signs and also trash cans where one can dump the bag with dog waste. In Carlsbad, San Diego, there are separate beaches where dogs are allowed. Hundreds of people take their dogs to the beach on weekends.

Some pet dogs are so small that people carry them in a bag. There are hundreds of small dogs being kept as their pets. There are also huge and scary-looking large dogs. People keep their dogs inside their homes. The dogs have their own beds and special food. People even buy insurance for their pets.

Coming from Nepal where people have a hard time feeding their children, seeing how many people keep dogs and cats as pets in this country was a new experience for me. They say it is harder to get into veterinary school than medical school. Veterinarians make good earnings and are also respected in the society.

Family Life and Educational Environment

The joint family system of Nepal makes it easy for students to go to school as long as they want. The parents and other family members bear the school expenses, and the student can live and eat with the family throughout their pursuit of education. The culture of studying and working at the same time has just entered Nepal. Some students from economically not-so-well-off families, and working professionals who want to advance their knowledge in their field have started grasping such opportunities.

In America and other Western countries, some students leave home after high school. If they want to go to college, they may have support from the family or apply for a student loan. There are different kinds of student loans available in the US. Many middle-class family parents struggle to cover the cost of the undergraduate years but consider their children's education to be their highest priority. When the first family member goes to college and has a successful career, this can influence the rest of the young people to follow his/her lead. Most American students are on their own to fund their graduate study. In Nordic countries, all levels of education are paid for by the people's high levels of taxation.

In America, many students work at least a few years after they complete their undergraduate degrees to gain experience and earn money for graduate study. Many students get some kind of scholarship, although the amount may not be sufficient. Most students in higher education also get some kind of loan to support their college or university education. Student loans are easily accessible, and many kinds are available. Student loan debt in America has been growing rapidly, reaching $1.41 trillion in 2019. Defaults on student loans are also growing every year, and creditors use debt collectors to collect the debts. Some states have started canceling licenses of those people who default on their payment—like driving licenses, nursing licenses, teaching certificates, and so on.

In Nepal, parents have their eyes on the students all the time, even after they cross their teenage years, though this is changing. In the US, college students go out and live on their own. They think of college as a place where they can feel free of their parents' watchful eyes for the first time, and they can experiment and enjoy their individualism and freedom. But now, because for financial reasons, more and more young people are staying with their parents even after graduating from college.

In America, the 1960s and 1970s were associated with drugs and sex and hippies. Nepal was also flooded with hippies around this time. Jhonchhe, known as Freak Street, near Hanuman Dhoka, was one of the centers for these hippies because of the many hotels, restaurants, and bars there. I saw men with long hair and both men and women wearing colorful clothes decorated with embroidery and beads and smoking joints of hashish. Many were interested in Eastern religions and meditation. America has changed, and the younger generations seem to be leaving this trend behind, but there are people who are still interested in the Eastern religions, meditation, and pot.

In America, due to financial constraints and the inability to find a lucrative job, more and more college graduates are going back to live with their parents until they find a proper job. Buying a house, getting married, and having children are a dream for most graduates. But since many have taken huge loans to finance their education, they have to put all this on hold.

Schools are divided into three different types according to grade or class. Elementary schools include kindergarten to sixth grade, middle school is grades seven and eight, and high school is grades nine to twelve. Schools may also be public, private, or charter schools. Charter schools are a mixture of both public and private schools, as they get some of their funding from the government but are run as private schools. As charter schools have no teachers' unions, teachers can be released or retained depending upon their performance more easily than in the public schools. Teachers' unions are very strong in America, so it is more difficult to discipline or fire teachers in public schools.

In America there has been much discussion about whether all high school graduates should go for higher education. High schools tend to prepare students to enter college, but not all high school graduates are interested in college. Students who do not want to go to college need to prepare themselves for vocational activities. There is little vocational education in the high schools.

High school graduation is a big milestone in the US, similar to our SLC in Nepal. The US Constitution allows American citizens to vote after the age of eighteen, and adulthood begins. Just before graduation the school arranges a "prom," or party, for students in the senior classes. Boys invite their girlfriends, or if they don't have a girlfriend, they ask some other girl to be their date. Some girls now invite boys. Students buy or rent formal clothes for the night and enjoy the night with a fancy dinner and dancing. A student can be invited to another school's prom if their girlfriend or boyfriend attends that school. The prom is often the first adult social event for teenagers.

The prom may also be considered a coming-of-age celebration. Different religious groups also have different coming-of-age celebrations, like the Jewish Bar/Bat Mitzvah, as a rite of passage into adulthood. This is like Nepal's Newars performing the *gufa rakhne* or *ihee* or *belbibah* ceremony for their daughters before their first menstruation, and almost all Nepali boys' *bratbandha* before the end of their teenage years.

Driving is an important skill in American life. Students usually get their driving license in their senior year in high school. Often the family provides a family car to the graduating student. The big cities of America have reliable and comfortable public transportation, but elsewhere, driving is a must.

American universities can be divided into three main categories. Public universities are funded by the government and usually have large enrollment, and tuition is lower than in private universities. State universities are funded by the state government by providing funds for students and research grants. Private universities are supported by tuition and donations from philanthropists, and the government does not provide any support except for some grants. Private universities charge higher tuition, and enrollment is much smaller than at public universities. There are also community colleges and universities, which charge reasonable tuition and other fees. In the nineteenth century, the US felt a need for practical higher education and gave huge plots of land to start universities and colleges to teach agriculture, engineering, and military science. These institutions of higher education are known as land grant universities. Some of them, like the Massachusetts Institution of Technology (MIT), Cornell University, and the University of Massachusetts, Amherst (UMass, Amherst) have become private universities.

The action against child abuse is another very strong part of the United States of America. The Federal Child Abuse Prevention and Treatment Act (CAPTA) requires certain individuals to report suspected child abuse. Municipalities also have a child abuse section in their offices. If they have any suspicion of child abuse or neglect on the part of the parents or the guardians, they will take away the child and put them in a child care center until the parents are allowed to take their child back. There are certain requirements for getting the baby back from the government custody. Even a teenager can call the government authorities if they feel they are not properly treated by their parents.

Law-Abiding Citizens on the Road

While preparing for my FSI language tester qualifying exam in my early Peace Corps days, I was listening to English-language materials. One skit featured a Venezuelan visitor to the US who was astounded by people stopping at a red light in the middle of the night when there was no sign of anyone on the road for miles. In Nepal people would not hesitate to drive through a red light if they didn't see anyone on the road. From the Venezuelan's and my own experience, this seems to be a problem in many developing countries.

My experience in America tells me that civilized people abide by laws whether there would be any consequences or not, with only a few exceptions. The law-abiding nature of the American people extends also to the four-way stop. It does not matter whether there is traffic on the road or not, everybody stops, looks or yields, and only then proceeds. A little more carelessness would certainly increase the number of accidents. If there is heavy traffic and there are vehicles coming from all four sides, the drivers automatically take turns, first come first go. If two cars stop at the same time, the one on the right goes first. No need for traffic police. Everybody is in a rush, but they wait until their turn comes. Can we imagine this kind of self-policing in Nepal?

Road transportation is the flesh and bones of the economic as well as the social life of America. Most people have at least one car, especially in places that lack good public transportation. Roads are very clearly marked with signs like Through Traffic Merge Left, Right Lane Must Turn Right, and HOV (high occupancy vehicles), vehicles with two or more passengers only. Speed limits are posted every few miles. White lines separating the lanes are very clear and look new and shiny everywhere. I don't know when they repaint them, since I have never seen anybody doing that.

I recently noticed signs saying "Traffic information: Turn on your radio if flashing." Traffic news is broadcast on a special radio station. If there is an accident that is causing a traffic jam, the radio announces the situation to alert drivers to take an alternative road to get to the destination—a good utilization of tax payers' dollars.

Unbroken double yellow lines on the left side may separate regular traffic from a lane for HOV vehicles. HOV lanes are created only in areas where traffic gets heavy when people are commuting to and from work. This is done to encourage people to car pool and thus save gas and reduce air pollution Only cars with two or more people can use this lane. I noticed a billboard in Southern California saying the minimum fine would be $341 for violators. People get big fines for their traffic regulation negligence in the US.

The Interstate Highway System was formed in 1956, and many local US roads were replaced by interstate highways for through traffic. Highways in some places are up to ten lanes wide and are busy all the time. There are roads especially for the convenience of commuters, such as Interstate 495 (I-495), which is 64 miles long, surrounds Washington, DC, and is also known as the Capital Beltway or just Beltway.

On several occasions I have seen people picking up trash from the roadside. Several years ago, I saw a man in his late sixties picking up trash on a major San Diego road. He had a stick about two and half feet long with a grabber on one end and a lever to open and close the grabber. This gentleman was casually dressed but did not look as if he was trying to profit from the trash. I was curious. One day I decided to talk to him. He said he was retired and that he picked up trash several days a week, just to pass his time as well as to keep the street clean. I later saw two ladies on another large road, also picking up trash with a grabber. Americans tend to like to volunteer to help the environment and other causes.

In America, people also tend to give equal importance to all kinds of work. They don't look down on you for doing manual work. I built up a casual friendship with two gentlemen in a local park who were there to take care of the grounds. I used to see them every day on my morning walk. Starting with good wishes in the morning, we would talk for a few minutes every day. After a while I started feeling I was missing something if I did not see them. This is in strict contrast with the situation in Nepal, where educated folk rarely interact with, for example, sweepers.

Taxes and Insurances

People give something to get something. Everybody, no matter how unselfish they are, has a wish to get something in return when they sacrifice their personal possessions, their time, or whatever that is that they are giving or donating. In some cases, the wish for something in return may not be for their own personal benefit. It could be for the betterment of society or for the betterment of humankind or something else. Bill Gates and Warren Buffett created their foundations based on their own beliefs. They get great satisfaction from helping others in accordance with their beliefs. The US government exempts nonprofit organizations from paying taxes, which also encourages investment in social causes.

Americans pay high taxes on their earnings—not the highest in the world, but a good proportion of their earnings as well as property tax and sales tax. But at the same time, they get good returns. Medicaid and Medicare (medical insurance for the poor and the elderly) are examples, along with the maintenance and upkeep of roads, bridges, and other infrastructure. Food stamps are for those with very low income, and unemployment insurance is another example.

In Nepal, tax money goes to pay the salary of civil servants, and we don't expect much else from the government. Nepali people would be happy if their tax money were not pocketed by civil servants, contractors, politicians, and others—whoever can get their hands on it.

We have personal experience in the proper use of tax dollars and an efficient insurance system. The mother of my son-in-law Pranaya was in Ho-Ho-Kus, New Jersey, one summer. While Archana and Pranaya were at work, she was making afternoon tea. Some hot water accidently spilled on Pia's (our granddaughter) arm. Worried and scared, not knowing what to do, she called Pranaya, who immediately called the emergency number, 911. An ambulance came, followed by a fire truck.

The paramedic looked at Pia's burn and decided it was a third-degree burn and must be treated in a hospital with full burn facilities. They called a helicopter and took Pia and her grandmother to a hospital that was a forty-five-minute drive from home.

Archana and Pranaya rushed straight to the hospital from work. Archana spent two nights with Pia in the hospital, and she was discharged on the third day. The ambulance and fire truck had arrived in less than five minutes. Apparently, they were required to use a helicopter if the burn hospital was more than fifteen minutes away. After Pia was discharged from the hospital, the fire department personnel visited her several times. Most of the hospital bills, ambulance charge, and everything else was paid for by the health insurance company. Archana and Pranaya paid a small portion of the bill. This is how efficiently the ambulance, fire department, and insurance system work in this country.

Oranges, Apricots, and Raspberries

The winter of 2011 was colder than usual in New Jersey, with intermittent snowstorms and rain. We stayed home most of the time except for a few grocery shopping trips, a few trips to museums and exhibitions, and some restaurant dinners.

In January 2012 we visited Jharana and her family in Carlsbad, near San Diego. The weather was warmer and more pleasant than in New York. On our way to Carlsbad from the airport, we saw trees loaded with tangerines on the roadsides, mainly at crossroads. After being in Carlsbad for a few weeks, we saw the fruits were still on the trees. It seemed nobody was interested in that fruit. The tangerines remained on the trees through April and May. Finally, they fell on the ground by the end of June. What a waste of good fruit! I could not figure out why people were not interested. People would go and buy the same kind of fruit from the supermarket, but here the fruit was rotting on the ground. Maybe it was protected by the government, as in a park where you are not allowed to take any flowers, or pine needles.

Similarly, in June we noticed apricot trees in public places laden with fruits with no one picking them. Then came raspberry season. During June and July, there were many berries that were red and ready for plucking. We didn't see anybody interested in these either. Was it just because they didn't have time to collect the fruit from the trees (and leave this work to farmers and low-level wage earners), or was it easier for them to buy from the supermarket? Or maybe the fruit trees were planted just for decoration. They really looked beautiful on the roadside. What about planting trees that would provide fruit as well as decorating the roadside?

The other attraction for us was *koirala* flowers (mountain ebony) of different colors, especially white and pink. This is a special treat in Nepal used to make curry or *achaar* (pickle/chutney). We saw trees laden with these flowers on the roadside, but people were not interested in them. What a waste!

The Conclusion

As I mentioned before, Will Newman, the country director of Peace Corps / Nepal in the early 1990s, was friendly and helpful to me throughout his tenure in Nepal. Our friendship continued even after both of us retired from the Peace Corps. We have kept in touch, and Kamala and I have visited Will and his wife Joyce frequently. On one of these visits, Will asked if I had thought of settling in America. He reminded me that he had encouraged me to apply for a special immigration visa when I was about to retire. In fact, that had never occurred to me. A village boy from Bandipur who had spent more than a decade in Chitawan teaching and pursuing other means of livelihood before finally coming to Kathmandu, I had thought my final destination was Kathmandu until I saw the possibility of moving to the US.

Even though I spend most of my time in the US now, I am still attached to Nepal. I travel back and forth between the US and Nepal, receiving great satisfaction whenever I am able to benefit the people of Nepal. As I mentioned previously, I continued working as an executive member of the board of directors for the Hospital and Rehabilitation Center for Disabled Children (HRDC) for more than three decades. I often expressed my intention to resign from that position so that another person could take over and perhaps have more time to spend helping physically disabled children. Each time, the board president, Dr. Ashok Kumar Banskota; the vice president, Mr. Krishna Prasad Bhattarai; and other executive members assured me that my assistance was valuable, however much time I could allot. So I continued this work to help disabled children.

My affiliation with HRDC provided me satisfaction and gave me peace. One incident stands out. It was the fall of 2008 when we were conducting a project involving a survey to measure our impact on the disabled children of Nepal, called "A Study of the Social Impact of Intervention Provided by the Hospital and Rehabilitation Center for Disabled Children." I was the project's coordinator. Two other members of our committee and I went to see one of our former patients in a remote part of Lalitpur district.

When we reached the patient's house, a woman was cleaning rice on the *pindhi*. When we explained who we were, tears rolled down her cheeks—she was sobbing. We worried that something might have gone wrong during her son's treatment. She soon collected herself and asked one of her sons to bring his brother home. They both came running home. Then she explained the story. It had been four years since she took her son to HRDC. The boy could not walk, but he crawled on all four limbs. The doctors at HRDC assessed him and performed surgery and provided all needed medications and physical therapy. A rehabilitation worker came to their house several times to check on him.

The boy had been playing soccer with his friends when we had arrived. His mother said she had never hoped for such a significant improvement. She told us that her tears were those of joy. She was glad to be able to express her gratitude toward all the members of HRDC who helped change her son's life. She was sure that if he had not gone to HRDC, he would still have been crawling, with very poor prospects for his future. Even if his mother had sold all her property, she would not have been able to take him for treatment to a private hospital, but HRDC did it free of charge knowing she was unable to pay. We were glad that the story had ended on such a positive note. HRDC charges are low for those who can pay and free to those who cannot pay.

This kind of outcome gives great satisfaction, and I am proud of whatever time I was able to spend with HRDC. I could also donate my time in the US, but I am able to provide a more useful service in Nepal. Hence, I continue to travel back and forth to Nepal. What keeps me coming back to the US is our grandchildren, all three of whom live in the US. Kamala and I regard them as precious gifts, and we like to spend as much time as we can with them.

From left to right:
Ambika, Kamala (my wife), Pranaya (Archana's husband), Pia (our grand-daughter), Archana (our younger daughter), Shreya (our granddaughter), Jhara-na (our older daughter), Ishaan (our grandson), Bob (Jharana's husband)

Glossary of Nepali and Newari Words Used in This Book

aamaa: Mother—kinship term also used for a mother figure

achaar: Pickle/chutney

aji: Grandma in Newari language

asar: Third month in Nepali Calendar

atmaa: Soul

baa: Father—kinship term also used for a father figure

babiyo: Grass used to make rope

bagedi: Small birds fried and eaten as appetizer

bahini: Sister

bahun kaathaa: A derogatory phrase used in Nepali hill towns to tease Brahmans

bar tree: A tree planted alongside with pipal tree in a chautari

bel bibah: A ceremony where Newar pre-adolescent girls are "married" to Bel fruit (Aegle marmelos)

bhat: Cooked rice

bhante: Buddhist priest

bhinaju: Older sister's husband

bhojpure khukuri: Gurkha knife made in Bhojpur

bratabandha: Coming of age ceremony for Nepali boys

byanjankaar: Chef

chamal: Uncooked rice

chapatti: Bread

charpi: Outhouse

chautari: A resting place on a trail with a big pipal and a bar tree

chhaupadi: Menstrual cycle, word mostly used in far-western hills

chilim: A clay bowl, a part of a water pipe, which contains tobacco

chitrakaar: Artist

chyaame: The untouchable Newari sweeper caste

dahi chiura: Yogurt and beaten rice

dal: Lentil

dal bhat: Rice and lentil (a typical Nepali meal)

dashain: Nepali festival celebrated to mark the victory of good over evil

dauraa suruwaal: Nepali national dress for men

dera: Apartment

deuda dance: Dance from far-western region of Nepal

deuki: Ancient practice of offering young girls to local temple

didi: Older sister

doko: A basket carried on person's back with the help of a head strap

ganja: Marijuana or hemp

ganja laagyo: Under the influence of marijuana

ghangar: A long skirt

ghantaghar: Clock Tower

ghee: Purified butter

gufa rakhne: Coming of age ceremony for Newari girls

gundri: Straw mat

guru: Teacher

guru mantra: Guru's teaching/ Sacred teaching

haat bazaar: Open market

haat mukh jodnu: To put hand and mouth together or to have enough
   to eat

habsi: A derogatory word used for black people

hakim: Boss

halawaai: Traditional confectioner

hukkah: An oriental water pipe used in smoking tobacco

hawan: Fire ritual

jand: Homemade beer made by fermenting millet or rice

jutho: Food or meal eaten (but not completed) considered impure

jwain: Brother-in-law or son-in-law

kali: Black woman

karuwa: Vessel for drinking water

ke garne?: What to do?

khaja: Snack

khukuri: Gorkha knife

koirala: Edible flower (Mountain ebony)

Kshatrias: The warrior or ruler caste

lagyo: Under the influence of alcohol/drug

maalaa: Garland

madhikarmi: Traditional baker

maile dekheko durbar: The Palace I Saw

mali: Gardener

mana: Measurement, equals to about fifteen pounds

mutthi: Fistful

mutthi dan: Fistful offering

namlo: Head strap sustaining a basket on the back

newar kode: A derogatory phrase used in Nepali hill towns to tease Newars

nhehnumaa beu: A Newari ritual performed on the seventh day of the death of a family member

pakauda: Fried vegetable snack

pindhi: A space outside the front door of a house, a patio

pipal: A big tree planted on a chautari (a resting place on the trail)

pirka: A low wooden seat

pradhan panch: Mayor

pranam: Respectful salutation

puja: Worship

puri tarkari: Fried bread and curry

purohit: Priest

radhi: Hand-loomed woolen rug

rajabhandari: Royal storekeeper

raj vaidhya: Royal Ayurvedic doctor

roti: Bread

saag: Spinach

saree: A garment elaborately draped around the body, traditionally worn by South Asian women

selroti: A traditional homemade donut-shaped rice bread

shisnu tarkaari: Curry made with the leaves of stinging nettle plant

shudras: The untouchable caste

sukuti: Dried meat

tarkari: Vegetable curry

thulo maanchhe: High-ranking official or a respected person in a village

tindhaaraa: A place where people get drinking water in Bandipur, it had three spouts but later two more were added

tomba: Fermented millet drink

topi: Traditional Nepali cap

tundikhel: Parade ground or play ground

ushina chamal ko bhaat: Parboiled cooked rice

vaidhya: Ayurvedic doctor

vaishyas: The traders or business people

wats: Buddhist temples in Thailand

Acronyms and Abbreviations

ADC—Aide-de-camp
AIC—Agriculture Input Corporation
APCD—Associate Peace Corps Director
BNA—Bandipures in North America
BSDC—Bandipur Social Development Committee
CAST—Center for Assessment and Training
CDO—Chief District Officer
CIA—Central Intelligence Agency
CIES—Council for International Exchange of Scholars
CNN—Cable News Network
COS—Close of Service
CPN UML—Communist Party of Nepal United Marxist Lennist
DC—District of Columbia
DEO—District Education Officer
ET—Early Termination
FSI—Foreign Service Institution
GSA—General Services Assistant
HBCU—Historically Black Colleges and Universities
HILT—High Intensive Language Training
HOV—High Occupancy Vehicle
HRDC—Hospital and Rehabilitation Center for Disabled Children
IIE—Institute of International Education
INGO—International Non-Governmental Organization

JFK—John Fitzgerald Kennedy
JTA—Junior Technical Assistant
MOE—Ministry of Education
NDS—National Development Service
NGO—Non-Governmental Organization
OSS—Office of Special Services
PCV—Peace Corps Volunteer
PSC—Personal Service Contract
PST—Pre-Service Training
PTSD—Post Traumatic Stress Disorder
RNAC—Royal Nepal Airlines Corporation
RPCV—Returned Peace Corps Volunteer
SEDU—Secondary Education Development Unit
SIT—School for International Training
SLC—School Leaving Certificate
SMT—Secondary Master Trainer
SSAT—Secondary School Aptitude Test
STOL—Short Take Off and Landing
TEFL—Teaching English as a Foreign Language
TCCU—Teachers College Columbia University
TOEFL—Test of English as a Foreign Language
TU—Tribhuvan University
USAID—United States Agency for International Development

References

Berman, J. (2009). "WHO: Waterborne Disease is World's Leading Killer." https://www.voanews.com/a/a-13-2005-03-17-voa34-67381152/274768.html

Joshee, A. (2015). *"Integrating Sustainable Development in Higher Education and the Financing Mechanism." A paper presented at the first international conference on Transformative Education Research and Sustainable Development, held in Dhulikhel and Organized by Kathmandu University, School of Education (KUSOED), Nepal and Murdoch University, School of Education, Australia.*

Shapiro, P. (1994). *A History of National Service in America.* Shapiro, Peter (ed.). Penn State University Library: Philadelphia

Made in the USA
Columbia, SC
14 October 2021

46990153R00163